fabulous Felt Hats

fabulous Felt Hats

Dazzling Designs from Handmade Felt

BY CHAD ALICE HAGEN

LARK BOOKS

A Division of Sterling Publishing Co., Inc.
New York

Editor: Joanne O'Sullivan

Art Director: Dana Irwin

Photographer: Sandra Stambaugh

Cover Designer: Barbara Zaretsky

Assistant Editor: Rebecca Guthrie

Associate Art Director:
Shannon Yokeley

Assistant Art Director: Lance Wille

Editorial Assistance:
Delores Gosnell

Library of Congress Cataloging-in-Publication Data

Hagen, Chad Alice.
    Fabulous felt hats : dazzling designs from handmade felt / by Chad Alice
Hagen.
        p. cm.
    Includes bibliographical references and index.
    ISBN 1-57990-542-0 (hardcover)
    1. Hats. 2. Felt hats. I. Title.
TT657.H34 2005
646.5--dc22

2005000177

10 9 8 7 6 5 4 3

Published by Lark Books, A Division of
Sterling Publishing Co., Inc.
387 Park Avenue South, New York, N.Y. 10016

Text and project designs © 2005, Chad Alice Hagen
Photography © 2005, Lark Books
Illustrations © 2005, Lark Books

Distributed in Canada by Sterling Publishing,
c/o Canadian Manda Group, 165 Dufferin Street
Toronto, Ontario, Canada M6K 3H6

Distributed in the United Kingdom by GMC Distribution Services,
Castle Place, 166 High Street, Lewes, East Sussex, England BN7 1XU

Distributed in Australia by Capricorn Link (Australia) Pty Ltd.,
P.O. Box 704, Windsor, NSW 2756 Australia

If you have questions or comments about this book, please contact:
Lark Books
67 Broadway, Asheville, NC 28801
(828) 253-0467

Manufactured in China

ISBN 13: 978-1-57990-542-2
ISBN 10: 1-57990-542-0

For information about custom editions, special sales, premium and corporate purchases, please contact
Sterling Special Sales Department at 800-805-5489 or specialsales@sterlingpub.com.

Contents

INTRODUCTION 6

GETTING STARTED 8
 MATERIALS 8
 TOOLS 12

FELTING BASICS 19
 BASIC BERET AND HOOD 26
 FINISHING TOUCHES 38

PROJECTS 42
 THE ARTIST BERET 44
 BE A STAR BERET 48
 QUEEN BERET 54
 SAILOR'S DELIGHT 58
 THE SNOOD 62
 SOPHISTICATED LADY 66
 BOB MARLEY TRIBUTE 70
 SPIKE 74
 THE KATHARINE HAT 80
 THE MADELINE HAT 84
 WINGED WONDER 88
 THE EXPLORER 92
 THE MEDIEVAL PEASANT 96
 SLICE AND DICE 100
 THE MARVELOUS MITRE 104

TEMPLATES 108
ACKNOWLEDGMENTS 111
BIBLIOGRAPHY 111
INDEX 112

INTRODUCTION

Beyond their practical purpose, hats make an undeniable personal statement. A baseball cap worn backward says one thing about its wearer, while an old-fashioned fedora says quite another. With so many options available, a hand-felted hat stands out as a sophisticated, powerful, and utterly creative choice of headwear. What makes a handcrafted hat so fascinating is the unique collaboration between the hat and the wearer. Some felt hats can stand alone as sculpture, but most are designed to come alive when placed on the head.

The wearer brings much to the process—positioning the hat at different angles, assuming different poses, taking on new personalities as the hat and head become one.

I had been making felt for years before I made my first hat. When I saw the fantastic felted hats made by Seattle felter, Jean Hicks, I knew I had to try this art form. I was totally intrigued by the combination of color, texture, and form that can come together in a hat. Years later, after making many strange hats and teaching others to make them, I'm still fascinated by the process.

Feltmaking is an ancient art, possibly the oldest textile technique known. Pieces of felt clothing and household objects, dated at over 6,000 years old, have been found in tombs wherever nomadic sheep herding was prevalent. Contemporary felters make wool into felt in almost the same way as their counterparts did thousands of years ago, and this connection to the past is one of the most satisfying aspects of feltmaking.

Transforming wool fibers into felted objects is simple, requiring not much more than hands and water to persuade wool to take its new form. Depending on the sheep breed that produces it, wool has various qualities, from drapable to stiff, or soft to harsh to the hand. Felters have endless opportunities for discovery and creativity. Hand-felted hats are a fascinating part of the history of felt. Throughout the years, they have served as indicators of rank and identity or as fashion accessories.

This book presents some of the hat forms I've taught in workshops in the United States, Holland, and England. I've found that it's one thing to teach someone how to make felt from wool, and quite another to show someone how to craft felt into wearable art. In addition to skill, discovery and the creative process are also essential components to making a successful felt hat.

The hats in this book are all, in one way or the other, variations on two basic hat styles: the beret and the hood, which I'll teach you how to make, step by step. The 15 hat projects in the book are imaginative interpretations of these forms, each altering the basic beret or hood, slightly or dramatically, for a very different look. Because of the non-woven nature of hand-felted wool, it can be cut without unraveling, stretched, folded, and molded into shapes. Appendages can be added during the felting process to create topknots, spikes, and wings. And the beautiful matte felted surface can be embellished with beads, buttons, felt designs, or even safety pins. Once you get comfortable with the techniques used to create these unique hats, you'll be able to improvise, imprinting each hat with your own unique style.

Felt hatmaking in the 1860s. PHOTO COURTESY OF BETH BEEDE

For further inspiration, I've included images of hats made by accomplished felters from around the world. With years of experience to their credit, these artists have created innovative, impressive designs that are a pleasure to look at and to wear.

As you're experimenting with making felt hats, you'll find yourself asking dozens of "What if...?" questions. When you come up with a new idea, try it at least once. Remember that there's no wrong way to make a felt hat. After all, you're not just making a hat—you're making a personal statement.

Some traditional felt hat forms

MATERIALS

Wool

It's the wool, of course, that makes hand-felted hats possible. Wool is composed of fibers covered with overlapping scales that help protect the fiber. When water is absorbed into wool, the inner cortex fibers swell, causing the scales to open outward, a process similar to the way a pinecone opens its scales. When wet wool is pressed or rubbed, the fibers move closer and closer together, appearing to shrink, and creating a densely entangled mass. This newly entangled mass is felt.

Types of Wool

Each breed and crossbreed of sheep grows a different type of wool. A lot of factors—including where a sheep lives, what it eats, and even its age—influence the quality of a sheep's fleece, and differences in quality (such as the thickness of the fiber, the size or number of the scales of the wool fiber, or the tightness of the crimp or curl) affect the felting ability of the wool and the end use of the felted wool.

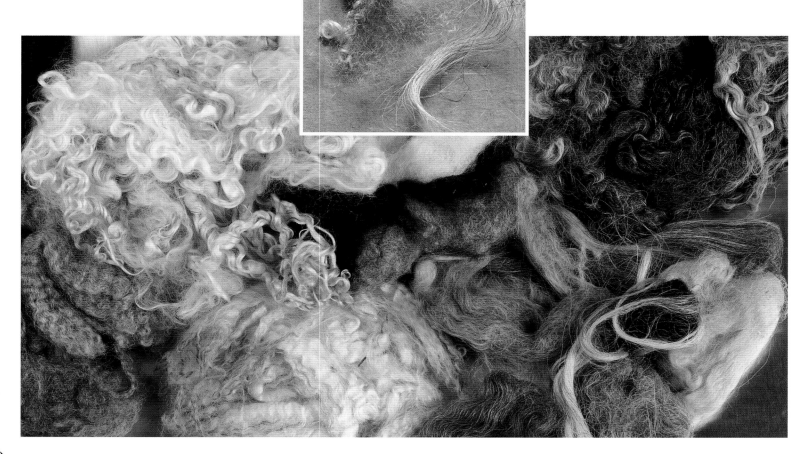

There are several informative books that cover the felting suitability of different wools. For the purposes of enabling you to jump right in to making a hand-felted hat, the wool choices have been made for you in this book—all the projects are made with either merino or Gotland wool. However, please experiment with different types of wool once you feel confident as a hatmaker.

Merino

Merino wool makes an extremely soft, pliable, and drapable felt. It's the perfect material for felt hats, for which softness is a premium. It takes a bit of patience and time to get used to the fineness of this wool, but the resulting hats will repay your perseverance.

Norwegian Gotland

Norwegian Gotland (referred to in this book as Gotland) wool has a thicker, coarser fiber, and is traditionally used in the Scandinavian countries and elsewhere for sturdy wearables, including hats. It makes very warm felt, so it's especially suited to wet and snowy climates. I wear a Gotland Katharine hat (see page 80) while teaching in Holland in the early spring. The hat keeps my head warm and totally dry even as I pedal my bike through rain and snow. When home, I just gently squeeze out the water, reshape the hat with a shake, and put it on a waterproof tray to dry.

Both merino and Gotland wools will shrink about 40 percent through the felting process. Both are also fast-felting wools, which makes them an excellent choice for beginners.

You'll need to order merino and Gotland wool from wool suppliers. See page 112 for information on how to find a list of suppliers.

GLOSSARY

Batt. 1) One form of cleaned and carded wool as it comes from a carding machine. Rectangular batts are built up of many thin layers of directionally aligned wool fibers. 2) The four perpendicular layers laid down on a pattern as you prepare to felt a hat.

Roving. The other form of cleaned and processed wool as it comes from a carding machine. A roving, also called a *sliver*, is a long, thick rope of wool fibers all aligned in the same direction.

Fulling. The hard felting that comes after the wool batt has been rubbed and pressed enough so that is has started to felt together. This includes throwing, squeezing, kneading, and vigorous rinsing under hot water.

Prefelt. Lightly felted wool that is sturdy enough to be cut into decorative shapes, but loose enough so that the wool fibers can easily felt with the unfelted fibers of the hat body.

Pat the bunny. Gently patting down the loose fibers that may stick up after you have laid out a shingle (see below) of wool.

Radiating layer. The fourth and outside layer of a beret batt. This layer is laid out in a pattern that radiates out from the center, rather than side to side or top to bottom.

Shingle. A very thin, even amount of wool that is pulled out from a roving. Shingles of wool placed side-by-side and end-to-end to build up a layer of the wool batt on top of a pattern.

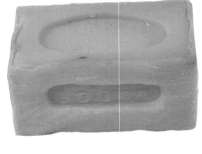

Soap

Combined in a solution with water, soap acts as a surfactant, helping the cortex of the wool fiber absorb water, which causes it to swell and its scales to open up. Soap also serves as a lubricating medium, helping wool fibers move around each other as you agitate them. At the beginning stages of felting, soap helps your hands gently glide over the surface of the wool without disturbing any fibers. Later, at the fulling stage (see page 35), soap prevents the felted surface from pilling as you rub it.

I prefer to use olive oil hand soap, many varieties of which can be found in health food and specialty stores. This type of soap is very kind to your hands—many of my students swear that their hands feel better after felting with olive oil soap. Another plus is that olive oil soap doesn't create massive amounts of suds like dishwashing detergents do. Olive oil soaps rinse out very quickly (even in cold water), and they usually have a higher pH value, which helps the wool's scales open out more.

While I have experimented with different ratios of soap to water, I feel best about the following three formulas. The first is a *basic soap gel*, made by chopping or grating a solid soap bar into water. The second solution, referred to as *soapy water* throughout the book, is used for wetting the dry felt at the beginning of a project. Soapy water is warm water mixed with a small amount of soap gel to help the water soak into the wool fiber cortex. The last solution, called *super soap*, is a concentrated solution made of half soap gel and half soapy water. It works wonders as you begin to rub and agitate the wool.

Any solution made of olive oil soap tends to break down pretty quickly once applied to wool, so you may need to reapply it as you work to maintain a good slippery feel.

Preparing the Basic Soap Gel

Chop up an 8-ounce (224 g) block of olive oil soap with a large knife or food processor. Place the small pieces in a 1-gallon (4 L) plastic container. Fill the container three-quarters full with hot tap water. Stir the mixture vigorously with a whisk. This is your *soap gel*. It will last for quite some time if the lid is kept slightly ajar to prevent mold. If the solution dries out or loses a lot of water to evaporation, just add more hot water and stir.

Grating soap for soap gel

Making Soapy Water

Fill another 1-gallon (4 L) plastic bucket to three-quarters full with warm water and add ¹/₂ cup (120 mL) of the soap gel. Use a whisk to blend the mixture very thoroughly. It should feel slippery when rubbed between your fingers.

Making Super Soap Solution

In a 1-pint (473 mL) container, add 1 cup (240 mL) soap gel to 1 cup (240 mL) soapy water. This super soap solution works well at the beginning of a felting project, after the excess water has been pushed out of the wool and you start to gently rub the wool. The solution may appear to be very gelatinous, but just spread it over the wool and start rubbing gently. Add more when the surface starts to feel unslippery and rough.
Note: If the felt surface starts to feel sticky, you're probably using too much soap. Add warm water until the surface feels more lubricated.

Water

The temperature and hardness of the water you use for felting will affect your results, so keep these factors in mind as you prepare to felt.

Wool will felt more quickly in warm to hot water, so use luke-warm (comfortable to the hand) water for wetting and felting. Use hot water (as hot as your hands can stand) when rinsing out the soap. Vigorous rubbing while rinsing with hot water further shrinks and tightens the wool fibers and creates a denser felt.

Hard water will react with your felting soap, forming curds or indissoluble matter that's hard to rinse out and reduces the lubricating power of your soap. You'll find you have to use much more soap to finish felting a project if you're using hard water. If you live in an area with hard water and don't have a water-softening device in your home, or if you're felting away from home and you don't know the hardness of the water, add ¹/₄ teaspoon (1.2 mL) of a water softener product to the water you use in both the soap gel and the soapy water solution.

Making super soap solution

Feltmaking doesn't require any specific tools. Almost anything can (and probably has) been used to make felt, at least once. Toolmaking is a very creative and competitive area for experienced felters who just love to invent new uses for common household and/or more exotic items. Some tools are developed for specialty felting, and some tools save time and labor. Some of

From left to right: head opening template, sushi mat, whisk, sponges, ridged plastic container lid, towels, scale, scissors, waterproof marker, ridged plastic sheet liner & non-skid mat (under other supplies)

these ideas have worked their way into the felting mainstream, but others seem to work only for the innovator who creates them. Hands are always the best tools for felting, but several helpful items used for making the hats in this book are included in our "felting kit."

Felting Kit

The materials lists for all the hats in this book call for a Felting Kit. Here's what's included.

Note: To save time, keep the felting kit items together in a bucket.

General Tools

- Safer than glass, plastic containers can be recycled from your kitchen or purchased. You'll need several 1-gallon (3.8 L) buckets for mixing the soap and soapy water.

- Buckets with lids and handles are ideal. Ice buckets are great for keeping soapy water warm longer.

- Small yogurt containers make great dipper cups, or you can order plastic safety beakers with spouts from dye or container companies.

- 1-pint (473 mL) containers are good for mixing the super soap solution.

- You can use dishwashing tubs or any other large container for waste water—just make sure the brim is low enough for you to squeeze water out of your projects comfortably.

- You'll need to keep five or six cellulose kitchen sponges. Let them dry out between felting sessions.

- Old hand towels are essential—keep several on hand.

- A kitchen whisk helps quickly mix soap solutions.

- Keep a sharp knife and chopping board or a food processor on hand to chop up the bars of soap.

- A 1-cup (240 mL) measuring cup with a long handle is useful for measuring out soapy water.

- You may also want to wear a waterproof apron to protect your clothes.

From left to right: juice can, large rubber bands, hat block, pot and plastic container (for shaping hats)

- A small calculator will help figure out shrinkage percentages. You'll need a black waterproof marker and a yardstick for drawing plastic resist patterns. A measuring tape is essential for hat and head measurements. Large, sharp sewing scissors will make cutting patterns and hat brims much easier. Keeping a pen and notebook next to your work area is helpful for jotting down sudden creative ideas and measurements. A small, inexpensive postage or food scale will be helpful to measure amounts of wool needed for various projects.

- A ridged plastic container lid is a valuable felting and hatmaking tool. You may have one in your cupboard, or you can check local secondhand stores.

- Clear, ridged, plastic shelf liner, paired with a non-skid sticky mat underneath makes a wonderful felt mat combination. Both are sold as shelf and drawer liners and can be found in hardware stores. This felting mat is used flat on your work surface, and is especially helpful when making topknots and for felting the brims of hats.

- A small bamboo mat used for sushi making (found in most Asian food stores) is a great tool for making topknots (see page 24).

- Your hands will always be your most useful tools. Your sense of touch will tell you how your felting is progressing before your eyes can even tell a difference. For this reason, try not to wear gloves. If the soap irritates your skin, experiment with soap alternatives. If you wear rings, take them off and put them in safe place, as protruding stones can rip soft felt.

Specialty Tools

There are two special tools I use when making hats that are shaped on hat blocks. One is the 46-ounce (1.3 L) juice can on which I place the solid hat block for pulling and stretching crowns and brims. The other tool is a large, wide rubber band (sometimes called a blocking tie) made from strips of rubber bicycle inner tubes. This band is pulled over the hat body for the final shaping on the block and keeps the felt stretched. It also marks the place where the brim will be turned.

Note: If you do plan to do a lot of felting, consider getting a thick, heavy-duty floor mat to stand on to relieve leg discomfort.

---

fELTING KIT

Several plastic 1-gallon (3.8 L) buckets	Sewing scissors
Dipping cup	Measuring tape
1-pint (473 mL) container	Waterproof marker
Dishwashing tub	Scale
1-cup (236 ml) measuring cup with a long handle	Calculator
5 to 6 cellulose kitchen sponges	Pen and notepad
2 to 3 hand towels	Ruler
Kitchen whisk	Ridged plastic container lid
Waterproof apron	Two-piece felt mat
	Sushi mat

Sewing Kit

A sewing kit is also a very useful hatmaking companion. You will want to use it for hand-sewing bias tape or adding beaded or embroidered embellishments.

A useful sewing kit will contain a box of large quilting pins (available at fabric stores). These pins have plastic or glass heads, which prevent them from getting lost in soft felt. A small pair of manicure scissors is great for snipping threads. A package of different-sized sewing needles (for hand-sewing), a few spools of sewing thread in different colors (especially black), a needle threader, and a thimble will meet most of your sewing needs. A measuring tape and sewing scissors (included in the felting kit) are also necessary. Hem clips, found in fabric stores, are great for holding the bias tape in place as you hand-sew. These clips are the same as the metal snap hair clips found in drug stores.

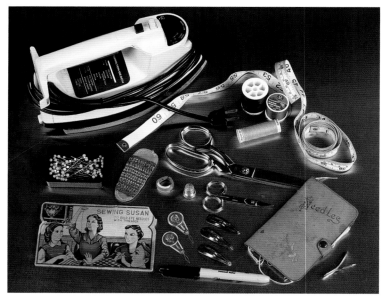

Clockwise from left: quilting pins, iron, measuring tape, thread, scissors, needles, marker, hem clips, thimbles

SEWING KIT

Plastic or glass head quilting pins	Hand-sewing needles
Sewing scissors	Needle threader
Manicure scissors	Measuring tape
Thread	Thimble
	Hem clips

Hat Blocks

Hat blocks are important for shaping hat patterns (called hoods in this book) into specific styles and sizes. While you can always use a kitchen pot or bowl, or even place the wet felt on your own head for shaping, the hat block is essential for repeating designs and consistent sizing. It makes the whole process much easier.

Early hat blocks were carved from wood, while later versions came in two (crown and brim) or more pieces. Some were made with adjustable spacers so a number of different sizes could be made from one style block.

Contemporary felt hatmakers have been rediscovering old wooden blocks in attics, antique stores, or on online auctions. They can be very expensive, and are probably better suited for

Polyurethane hat blocks

Hat blocks made from recycled automobile plastic

display than for everyday use (the soap and water used in the hatmaking process will damage the wood unless it's covered with plastic while in use).

A yellow, smooth-coated, solid polyurethane hat block, sold as a straw hatmaking form is a great choice. It comes in four different styles (flat top, round, and tall/dome styles are used in this book) and three common hat sizes: 21, 22, and 23 inches (53, 56, and 59 cm). You can pin into them, making it easier to precision-cut crowns. They're lightweight and inexpensive. One drawback to these hat blocks is that there's a paper label glued to the bottom of the block. When the paper becomes wet, it peels off in small pieces that tend to get into the wool fibers, and are hard to remove. It's much easier to soak the bottoms before the first use, then scrub off the label with a brush.

You can also find a Danish-made, heavy-duty, polystyrene block that can be attached to a wooden support, which eliminates the need to use a juice can under the hat block. There's only one style available in this type of block, but one can be endlessly creative.

One of my favorite types of hat blocks is made from recycled automobile plastic. These very hard and durable forms can't be pinned into, but can be used for both hand-felting and steaming hats. They come in over 30 different styles, including children's and doll sizes, and all styles come in five or more sizes. The Madeline Hat (page 84) is an example made from a flamenco-style hat block made from this material. Custom sizing and shaping is available. The brim is attached to the crown, so stretching the crown can be a bit problematic.

Sources for all these types of hat blocks can be found by following the link listed in the Supplies list on page 112.

Plastic Resist Patterns

You'll need a plastic resist pattern for most hats you make. It's very simple to measure and cut out patterns, and you can use them over and over again.

There are several materials you can use for a plastic resist pattern. My personal favorite is a thick foam sheet that's often used as packing material. You can reuse material you got in a package, or check packing stores for wide sheets of this material. Thin bubble wrap or dense craft foam found in craft stores are other good options. The largest size craft foam sheet commonly available is 10 x 12 inches (25 x 30.5 cm), so you would be limited to a small pattern.

Thick material is a good choice because you can feel the edge of the pattern more easily when you're laying out the wool, and thicker material usually eliminates the ridge formed at the edge of the pattern when the resist is taken out of the hat.

Heavy 4 to 6 mm plastic (found at hardware stores) or heavy vinyl (found at fabric stores) are other options. Also consider smooth-backed oilcloth, or in a pinch, cotton fabric. Cotton fabric tends to stick to wool fibers and can distort the fragile felt when removed from a hat. Some felters like to use the waxed cardboard used for food packaging, or even corrugated cardboard. Cardboard will only last for a few uses, though, and the other materials described are much more durable.

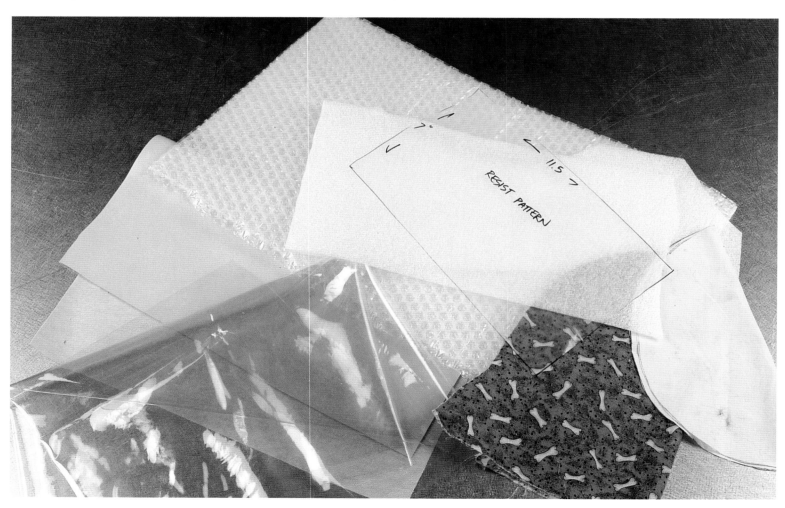

Making Plastic Resist Patterns

You Will Need

Your choice of plastic resist material
Waterproof marker
Scissors
Measuring tape
Ruler
Calculator
Photocopier

Beret Pattern

The diameter of the circle you create determines the style of beret. A 10-inch- (25.4 cm) diameter circle makes a skullcap. A 12-inch- (30.5 cm) diameter circle creates a form-fitting beret and serves as the foundation for a banded beret. A 14-inch (35.6 cm) circle makes a larger beret which can be pulled down over the ears. Larger diameters make for interesting designs and wearing solutions. No matter what size pattern you make, the size of the head opening is always the same: a 5-inch (10 cm) circle. This opening can be enlarged or reduced during the finishing stages of making the beret.

We'll use a 12-inch- (30.5 cm) diameter pattern as an example. Each project in the book will include a specific size for your pattern.

Place your ruler on the resist material and place a mark at 0 inches (or at the end of the ruler), 6 inches (15 cm), and 12 inches (30.5 cm). Rotate the ruler in a circle, placing a mark where the ruler ends and at 12 inches (30.5 cm). Place marks every 1 inch (2.5 cm), moving around in a circle. Connect the marks, cut out the resulting circle. This is your plastic resist pattern.

Hood Pattern

The hood or cone pattern is used to make close-fitting brimless caps, and small and large brimmed hats. The hood patterns used in this book are provided for you (see pages 108 to 110). Copy and enlarge the pattern by the percentage noted:

Most adult head sizes range between 21 and 24 inches (56 to 61 cm). The hood patterns are designed for a 22 to 23-inch (58.5 cm) head size. Although you may successfully use the pattern at the recommended enlargement for any size, you can also make the pattern slightly smaller or larger.

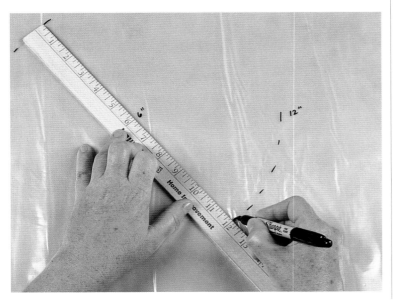

Drawing a beret pattern

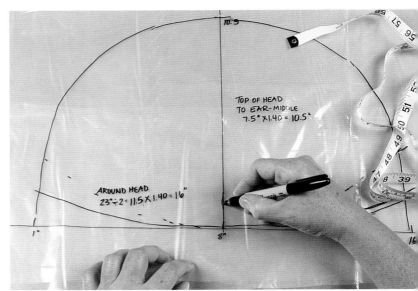

Drawing a hood pattern

Drawing Your Own Hood Pattern

The hood pattern is based on the following head measurements.

■ The distance around the head at the largest point. (Don't forget the bump at the lower back of the head. I also like to stick my finger under the measuring tape to allow for ease.)

■ The distance from the top of the head to the middle of the ears.

You can plot the hood shape with these measurements. Each measurement needs to be increased by the shrinkage percentage of the wool. Both of the wools we will be using (merino and Gotland) for the projects in this book will shrink about 40 percent.

■ Take the head circumference measurement and divide it in half. Multiply that number by 1.40 (for shrinkage). The resulting measurement represents the bottom line of your hood pattern. Measure and draw the bottom line (A), and mark its center (B^2).

■ Take the top to ear measurement, and multiply that number by 1.40 (for shrinkage). The resulting measurement represents the line you'll draw up from the center point (B^2B^1).

■ Connect the three points (AB^1A) with a graceful curve.

■ Measure down from the top center point along the curve for the same distance as the center line. Draw another gentle curve (DB^2D) from the two side marks to the bottom center. This is your hood or cap pattern.

■ To add a brim, measure the desired width of the brim (E) down from the curved bottom line (DB^2D) of the cap. Flare out the sides of the brim.

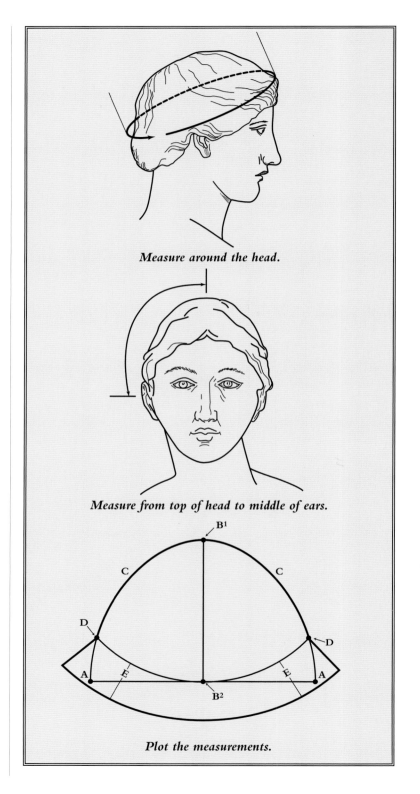

Measure around the head.

Measure from top of head to middle of ears.

Plot the measurements.

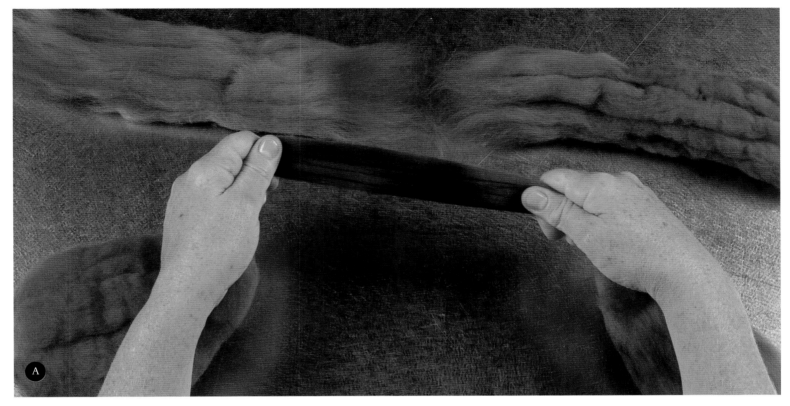

A.

Laying Out the Wool

The wool you'll use to make the hats and berets in this book will come already processed. This means that the wool has been washed and cleaned of all vegetable matter, dirt, and oils, and has been put through a carding machine that straightens and combs the wool fibers so they are all laying in the same direction. The wool is taken off the carding machine in either roving (a thick rope of wool wound into "bumps") or batts, flat rectangles of very thin, multiple layers of wool.

This section of the book will show you how to lay out either the roving or batt wool to form the thin, even layers that are the foundation of each hat or beret. Learning to lay out wool layers will help you make beautifully even and flat felt, but it takes a bit of practice, time, and patience. If you're not familiar with working with wool, take your time and work with small amounts of the wool at a time. Trying to rush a project by using long, thick pieces of wool will only create uneven felt.

Laying Out Merino Roving

A. For this introduction to laying out merino roving layers, you will need a 24-inch (61 cm) merino roving.

As shown in photo A, place your hands about 5 to 6 inches (13 to 15 cm) apart. Gently pull the merino roving into equal halves, resulting in two 12-inch (30.5 cm) rovings. Make sure the roving is not twisted because even a single twist makes it almost impossible to pull the wool apart. **Note:** The term "pull," refers to pulling the roving apart lengthwise. The term "divide" refers to splitting the roving in half widthwise.

B. Visually estimate the center, and divide one of the 12-inch (30.5 cm) lengths cleanly into equal halves with your thumbs and forefingers. Divide those two halves again, creating four thin lengths of roving.

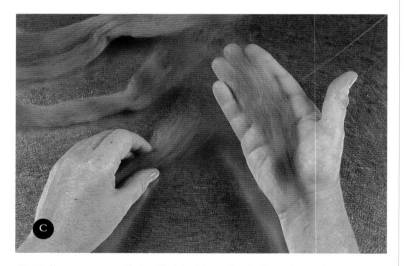

C. Pull apart one of the divided lengths in lengths as long as your hand. This is the size and amount of merino wool that you will use when laying out "shingles" (pieces of wool that are arranged in layers).

Note: If left-handed, reverse the hand instructions.

D. Hold the small length of roving in your right hand, pinched between your thumb and side of your forefinger. Lay the other end of the roving on the table, and place the forefinger of your left hand flat over the very end of the roving. Hold this finger down as you pull out a very thin, even shingle of wool with your other hand. Pat this shingle down very gently with your hand before proceeding with the next step. This process is called "patting the bunny."

Continue to lay out small, thin shingles of wool side by side in the same direction, overlapping the thin tops and bottoms like shingles on a roof, until you have covered the area required for your project. If you have wool left over, go back over the layer, "patting the bunny" until you feel areas that may need more wool. Use all the wool designated for that layer.

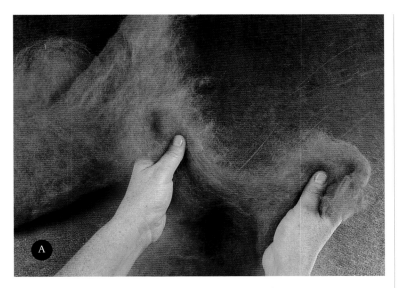

Laying Out Gotland Batts

A. Since wool batts may vary in thickness, I lay out batt wool this way: Unroll the entire batt, and tear it into 1-foot (30.5 cm) wide sections. You will notice that the batt tears much more easily in the direction of the carded fibers.

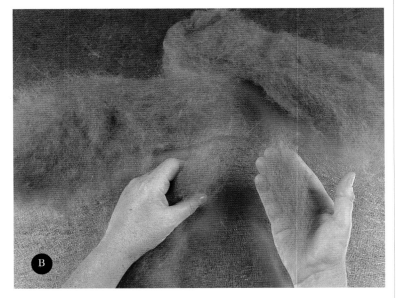

B. Take one of the sections you just tore, and tear it into hand-sized pieces. This is the amount of the fiber you'll need when laying out the wool.

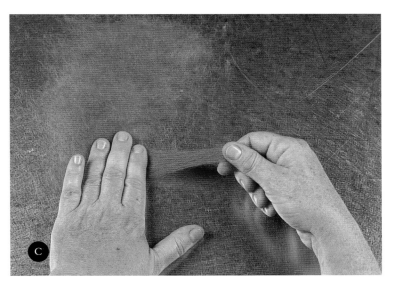

C. Hold half of the hand-sized piece in your right hand, and lay the other half on your work surface. Use the flat surface of your left hand to hold down the end of the wool, and gently pull it with your right hand. You will get a good-sized shingle. Pat the bunny as described on page 20. Continue to pull out the shingles, overlapping end to end and side to side in the same direction to cover the required area.

For Both Merino Roving and Gotland Batts

Always pat each new shingle down before moving on. If you remember to pat the bunny after laying down each piece of wool, you will not have as many problems with floating bits of wool catching on the wool in your hands. It also helps to condense the fibers and accustom your hand to the feel of the layers.

Laying Out Layers

For the projects in this book, you'll need to lay out four layers of wool for the hat bodies and prefelts (see right column) using the process described on pages 20 and 21. Each hat project will specify the amount of wool needed. It's important to remember that each layer is laid down perpendicular to the previous layer: the first and third layers are laid out right to left; and the second and fourth layers are laid out top to bottom. This builds up strength in the wool batt.

Troubleshooting

As you lay out layers, check to see if there are any "hills" (areas with too much wool) or "valleys" (skimpy areas) in your layer. The first layer should be thin enough that you could almost read a newspaper through it. You may go back and lay down additional shingles to make layers more even. If there are thicker shingles in your layer, don't try to pick at them, just try to be more even next time.

Making Prefelt

Prefelt is lightly felted wool, often used to add designs to a hat. It's sturdy enough to be cut into shapes, but loose enough so that the wool fibers can easily felt with the unfelted fibers of the hat body.

Several of the hats in this book include prefelt designs felted to the hat body (Be a Star Beret, page 48; Bob Marley Tribute, page 70; The Medieval Peasant, page 96; and The Explorer, page 92) but you may add them to any hat design you wish. The materials list for each project will specify amounts and colors of wool needed.

Making Prefelt Designs

Take the wool needed for your prefelt design and divide it into four sections, one for each layer that you'll lay out. Lay out the wool as described on pages 20 and 21. Continue laying out layers as described in the column on the left.

After all four layers are laid out, fold over the wispy edges. Gently wet the entire surface of the prefelt with soapy water. Press down with open fingers to saturate the wool. Alternate pressing and rubbing the entire surface *very gently*. You should rub so gently that it will feel like your hands are moving on the

Tip

After you have placed your prefelt designs on the first side of the hat body, place a large piece of plastic over that side. Flip the plastic and hat body together to help keep all the wet design pieces on the hat.

surface of the soap bubbles. No fibers should be moving under your hands. Always add more super soap solution (see page 11) when the wool stops feeling slippery. The soap solution breaks down pretty quickly and will need to be replaced often.

Continue to alternate rubbing and pressing until the batt feels more solid, like a fabric. You should be able to drag your fingers across the surface without moving any fibers. Gently rinse the batt under cool water, squeeze dry, and lay flat on the table.

Trace your designs onto the prefelt with a marker. (The ink will wash off during the felting process.) You can cut your designs from the wet prefelt, but it may be easier to wait until it's dry.

Attach the prefelt designs to the hat as described in the instructions for your specific project.

Prefelted wool

23

Making Topknots, Dreadlocks, Tails, and Spikes

Many of the hat designs in this book feature a topknot or tail. Some of the topknots are one color and pretty simple to make. Other designs may call for stripes or just a small bit of color on the tip. Some topknots are long, some very short, and some hats will have dozens of them.

Determining the Thickness of Your Topknot

The materials list for each project will provide the amount and color of wool needed for your topknot, and a suggested length and thickness, from one-half roving to one-eighth roving thickness.

■ Dividing the length of roving evenly in half makes a half-roving thickness.

■ A quarter-roving thickness is made by dividing the length of roving in half again.

■ A one-eighth roving thickness is made by dividing the quarter-rovings.

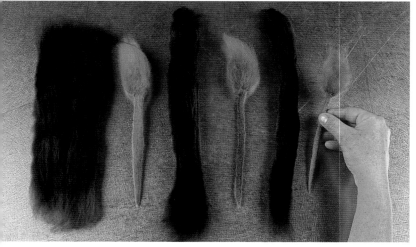

Left to right: half-roving thickness, quarter-roving thickness, one-eighth roving thickness

Once you've got the wool divided to the correct thickness, lightly roll the dry wool back and forth a few times on the felt mat to compress the fibers. The bottom 2 inches (5 cm) is called the "root."

Keep the root dry as you dip the rest of the roving into soapy water. Squeeze the wool several times to thoroughly soak the fibers (still keeping the root dry). Very gently roll the wet top-knot back and forth a few times to get it into a round shape and start the fibers felting.

Gently squeeze out the excess water and continue to roll the topknot on the felt mat, moving your outstretched fingers from the root to the opposite end until the topknot becomes very firm. You may also use the sushi mat at this point to speed up the felting.

The dry fibers of the root should be as long as the palm of your hand. Tear off any excess. Open out the dry fibers of the root into a circle, then tug the beginning of the felted part of the topknot.

Making a Curled Topknot

To make a twisted or curled topknot, twist the roving around a dowel and fasten it with a rubber band. Let the topknot dry before untwisting (see photos A and B below).

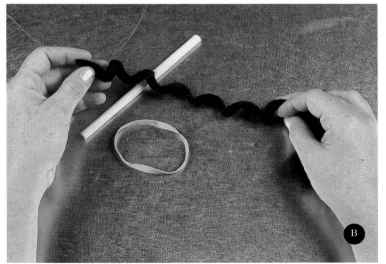

BASIC BERET & BASIC HOOD

The Artist Beret (page 44), Be a Star Beret (page 48), Queen Beret (page 54), Sailor's Delight (page 58), and the Snood (page 62) are all based on the Basic Beret. You don't need a hat block or special tools to make it, and merely changing the shape and size of the resist pattern can result in hundreds of variations. Changing the placement or style of the head opening will dramatically change how the beret sits on the head. Adding a band to the head opening creates an entirely new look, while reshaping the basic beret while still wet creates elegant sculptural effects.

The hood-shaped hats—Sophisticated Lady (page 66), Bob Marley Tribute (page 70), Spike (page 74), Katharine (page 80), Madeline (page 84), Winged Wonder (page 88), Explorer (page 92), Medieval Peasant (page 96), and Slice and Dice (page 100)—are all formed on hat blocks to give them their characteristic profiles. As with the berets, there are many, many variations that will create exciting new shapes. Adding a brim—curved up or down, flat, large or small, evenly cut, or asymmetrical—creates an entirely different shape. Adding topknots, dreadlocks, spikes, wings, or cutting into the felted wool changes the look even more.

These instructions will take you through the entire hatmaking process. To make beret-based hats, follow steps 1 through 23. To make hood-based hats, follow the steps for the beret, except when a step specifies different instructions for the hood, as indicated by a star and the color yellow. Steps 24 through 29 apply to the hood only.

For each hat, detailed materials lists (specifying the amounts and colors of wool needed and other items) are found in the project section of the book. You'll find plastic resist pattern templates for hoods on pages 108 through 110.

Beret-Based Style

Hood-Based Style

■ You Will Need

Merino roving or Gotland batt

Soapy water (page 11)

Felting kit (page 12)

Plastic resist pattern (page 17)

Cardboard circle, 5-inch (13 cm) diameter (for the beret head opening template only)

Hat block (for the hood only)

Small plastic container lid (for the hood only)

Large rubber band (for the hood only)

46-ounce (1.3 l) juice can (for the hood only)

Notes

Both the beret and the hood will be referred to as the "hat" in these combined directions, except where directions are specific to either type of hat.

Projects can be stopped and restarted at any time during the process. If your project is mostly felted and you can't finish it, gently rinse the soap out in cool water and lay the hat on a rack to dry. Don't leave a wet project sitting for more than a few hours. Cover the project with plastic if animals or children will be in your work area. When you return, rewet the wool with warm soapy water.

Refer back to the Laying Out the Wool on page 19 before starting your project.

Keep your posture straight, and try to avoid bending your hands at the wrist. If you're prone to carpal tunnel syndrome, you may want to raise up your worktable to a good working height, about 2 inches (5 cm) below your bent elbow.

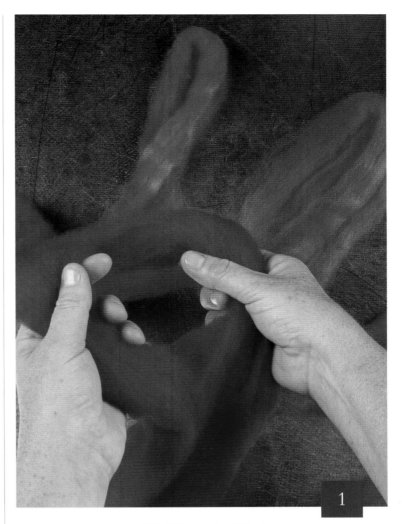

Dividing the Wool

1 Divide your wool into two piles of equal size. Each of the piles will be made into a layered batt. If you're making a beret, one batt will be used for the top of the hat, the other for the bottom. If you're making a hood, one batt will be used for each side. For now, set one pile of wool away from your work area. Divide the remaining pile into four equal sections. Each one of these sections will be used for one layer of the wool batt.

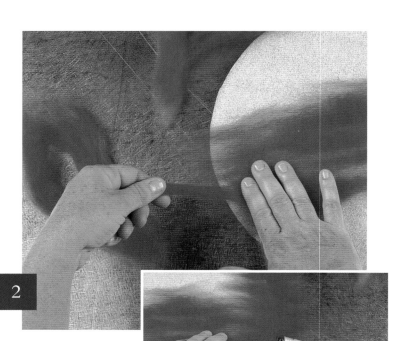

2

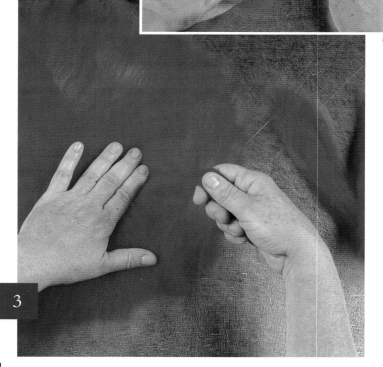

3

Laying Out the Wool

2 Place the plastic resist pattern on your work surface. Pick up the first section of the wool you divided. Lay out a thin layer over the resist pattern, moving from left to right and letting the wool extend about 2 inches (5 cm) beyond the edges of the resist pattern to create the seam. Use all of the first section of divided wool to complete the first layer and remember to "pat the bunny" (see page 20).

Note: The seam area is the 2 inches (5.1 cm) of wool that extends beyond the edges of the resist pattern. If you are laying out wool from left to right, the seam will be on the left and right sides of the plastic pattern. When you lay out the wool from the top to the bottom of the pattern, you will extend the seam wool on the top and the bottom.

3 The second layer is laid out perpendicular to the first layer, using the second section of wool. For the third layer, use the third section of wool, laying out the wool perpendicular to the previous layer. With each layer, remember to extend the wool about 2 inches (5 cm) beyond the resist pattern for the seams.

4 For the hood, the fourth layer (using the fourth section of wool) is laid out perpendicular to the third layer. Repeat each step for the second pile of wool (the one you set aside in step 1).

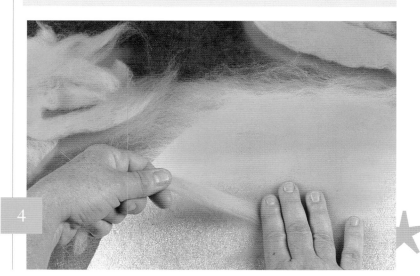

4

4 For the beret, the fourth layer (using the fourth section of wool) is laid out in a pattern that radiates out from the center. Lay out a strip of wool from edge to edge across the center of the pattern. Lay out another strip of wool perpendicular to the first. Fill in the sections between, laying the wool from the center out to the edge. Extend the wool 2 inches (5 cm) around the entire edge of this layer. Repeat each step for the second pile of wool (the one you set aside in step 1).

Plucking the Wool

5 When you're finished laying out both batts, make sure that the seam extends enough on all sides by placing the plastic resist pattern on the center top of the batt and measuring the width of the outside seam. If some areas are wider than 2 inches (5 cm), press down firmly on the resist with one hand and gently pluck off the longer pieces of wool. If areas are too narrow, build them up with additional wool.

Dry Felting

6 Once the wool is laid out in the four layers, a technique called "dry felting" can be used to condense the fibers, making them stick together and starting the felting process. This process makes it much easier for you to move the batt from place to place as you work. It also shortens the wet felting time, since it helps press the wool together.

To "dry felt," place your open hands on the dry felt batt and gently move the area under your hands up and down against the table for about 10 seconds. Move your hands carefully to the next area, and repeat the motion, systematically covering the entire batt. You'll notice a difference in the batt immediately.

Turn the batt over, remove the plastic resist pattern, and place it in a safe spot away from your work space. **Note:** Place the batt on a large piece of cardboard to help move it.

Repeat steps 2 through 6 for the second batt.

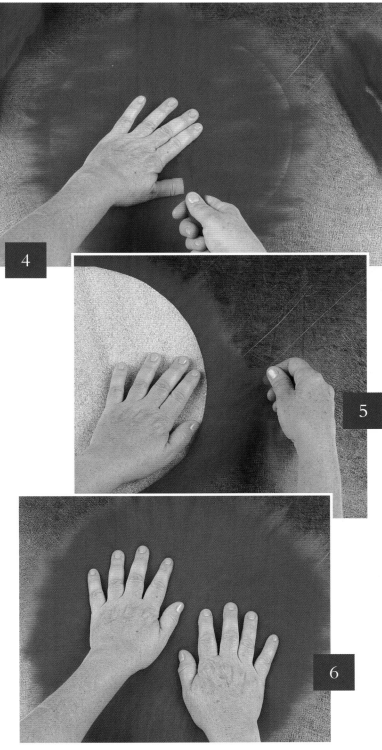

Wetting the Batts

7 For the hood, place one batt in front of you, horizontal side down. For the beret, place the radiating side down, with the plastic resist on top. Place the plastic resist in the center of the batt. Note the location of the edge of the resist (2 inches [5 cm] from the edge of the wool)—this is the seam line.

8 Fill your large water bucket about three-quarters full of warm soapy water (see page 11). Whisk the solution well, as the soap tends to settle to the bottom of the bucket. Remove the resist and, with a dipper full of the soapy water, gently dribble a line of water on the seam line. Don't get the outside seam wool wet. Crisscross the area inside the circle with about two more dippers full of soapy water.

9 Place the resist pattern back down over the wet wool and gently press with your hands, wetting the whole area underneath the resist pattern. You'll know the wool is saturated when it feels like it's sticking to the table surface and you don't see any more air bubbles through the plastic resist. If you need to add more water, pick up the edge of the plastic resist and dribble it on. Just be sure to keep the seam area dry.

10 For the hood, pull up the bottom edge of the plastic resist pattern. Notice the line between the wet and dry wool. This is the "waterline." Fold up the dry seam wool on the waterline and press down. Replace the plastic resist pattern and press down with your fingers over this area to wet it thoroughly. This is one side of the head opening of your hood. Gently fold the other dry seam area over the plastic resist pattern. You can tack down stubborn areas with small drops of soapy water. Keep the seam area as dry as possible to maintain a good connection with the other side of the hood.

30

10 For the beret, gently fold the dry seam edges over the resist pattern. It's easiest to do this with the back of your hands so you don't pull the seam wool, weakening the seam. You may tack down stubborn areas with small drops of soapy water. Keep this area as dry as you can so the wool will connect well with the other side of the beret.

11 Pick up the other batt (radiating side up for the beret, horizontal side up for the hood) folding it in half for easier handling. Center it directly on top of the bottom batt. Press down gently.

12 Since you won't be able to see the resist pattern at this stage, remember that your seam line is 2 inches (5 cm) from the outside edge. With your dipper full of soapy water, dribble a line of water on the seam line. Dribble an additional three dippers of soapy water over the wool inside the circle. Press your fingers down directly on the wet wool to saturate. Press, don't rub, your way to the edge of the resist. You will be able to feel a drop off that marks the edge of the resist pattern. Continue to work your way around the edge of the resist, adding more soapy water if you need to, remembering to keep the outside 2-inch (5 cm) seam dry.

Note: When pressing down on the wet wool, use only your open, flat fingers. If you use your whole hand, the palm of the hand will form a vacuum and suck up the wet fibers as you raise your hands off the surface. Open up your fingers so the soapy water can rise between them. The purpose of pressing down is to move the soapy water through the wet wool.

Flipping Over the Hat

13 With your pincher fingers (thumb and index finger of each hand), grab the top corners of the batt firmly. Remember that the wool is wet and heavy and the plastic resist is slippery. With one quick, smooth motion, pick up the entire batt high enough that the bottom seam doesn't fold over, and flip it over to the other side.

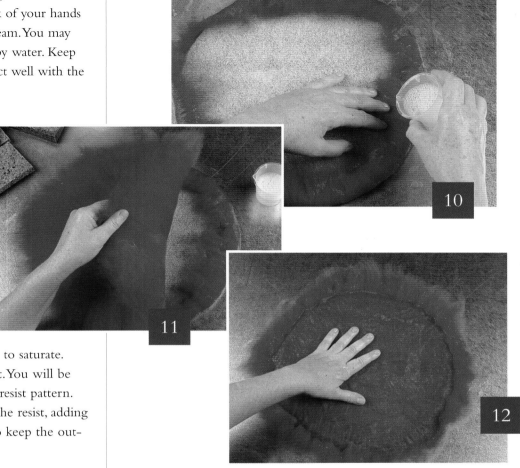

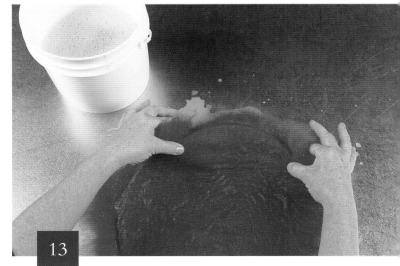

14 For the hood, pull up and fold back the head-opening side, making sure that you include both the plastic resist pattern and the wool that's wrapped around it. Fold the head opening seam wool up along the waterline and press down to wet. Replace the plastic resist. Fold the remaining dry seams down on the wet hat body, pressing to saturate.

14 For the beret, fold the dry seam edge down onto the wet felt, pressing to wet it. Your beret now should look like round pizza dough!

Attaching Topknots, Dreadlocks, Spikes, or Prefelt Designs

15 Now is the time to add any topknots, dreadlocks, spikes, or prefelt designs onto the hat body. Each project will provide specific instructions. **Note:** Attaching topknots and dreadlocks is easier if you rub them between your fingers.

Pressing Out Excess Water

16 Place five or six sponges about 2 inches (5 cm) from your batt to soak up excess water. Don't place the sponges any closer as they will soak up too much water. When the sponges become saturated, squeeze them out in the wastewater tub.

Start moving the water out by *pressing* your open, flat fingers straight down on the wet hat so that water and soap bubbles come up between your fingers. It's OK to press down pretty hard. Systematically press your flat fingers over the entire surface of the hat, starting at the edge furthest away from the sponges. Work your way toward the sponges, moving the excess water ahead of your fingers. Don't rub, just press down. Press and hold your hands down for a few seconds at the sponge edge so that the excess water will be absorbed by the sponges. Repeat the water-pressing process several times, squeezing out the sponges into the waste-water tub in between. When you can press your fingers down hard on the hat and just a little soapy water rises above the wool surface, you're ready to start the rest of the felting process.

Gently dribble and spread the super soap solution (see recipe on page 11) over the hat. Alternate pressing and rubbing the entire surface of the batt *very gently*. Rub so gently that it feels like your hands are moving on the surface of the soap bubbles. No fibers should be moving under your hands. Move your hands in inward circles so that you don't rub the seams off the hat. Always add more super soap solution when the wool stops feeling slippery. The super soap breaks down pretty quickly once on the wool and needs to be replaced frequently.

17 Continue to alternate rubbing and pressing until the wool feels more solid, like a fabric. You should be able to drag your fingers gently across the surface without moving any fibers. When this happens, flip over the hat. Remember that this new wool surface is still very fragile. Add super soap and continue pressing and gently rubbing as you did with the first side of the hat until the second side achieves the same texture. As the fibers become more condensed and the hat feels sturdier, you can rub a bit harder, always keeping your eye on the surface, making sure that the fibers aren't moving. Add more super soap solution when necessary.

Creating the Head Opening

18 The head opening has already been formed for the hood. Gently open the bottom of the hat, pulling sides apart if they have felted together a bit. Reach into the crown of the hood, grab the edge of the resist pattern, and pull it out.

18 Now it's time to cut the head opening and take out the resist pattern. Place the cardboard circle template on the correct location for the head opening, and carefully cut out the circle of felt. Avoid cutting through the resist pattern inside the beret.

Reach inside the beret, grab the edge of the resist pattern, and pull it out. Rub the cut opening with soapy water for about 1 minute to help prevent stretching. **Note:** The size of the head opening (5-inch [13 cm] diameter) is always the same, no matter how big or small your head may be.

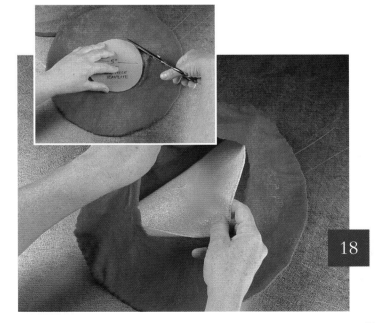

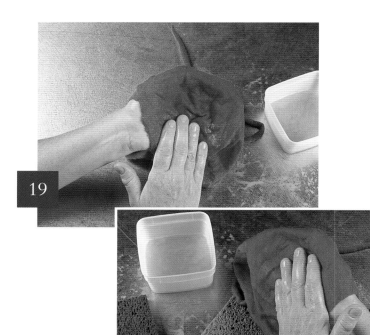

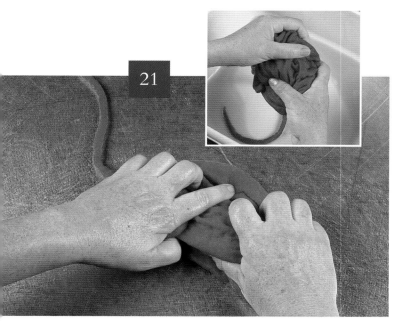

Smoothing the Resist Edge

19 As you removed the resist, you may have noticed a ridge or bump along the outside fold of the hat. This ridge is caused by wool fibers sliding off the edge of the resist pattern. A thicker resist material will create less of a ridge and vice versa. To smooth out this ridge, add lots of soapy water, place one hand inside the hat, holding your palm open under the ridge area, and gently rub the ridge with your other hand. Let the weight of the hat rest on the table. If the ridge is large, try gently stretching it open with your fingers first. If you rub too hard without stretching the ridge open, you might felt it permanently into a bump. Work the ridge this way until it disappears. **Note:** Place sponges under the hat to absorb the water that will drip during this process.

Felting the Hat

20 Use the length of your hand (from the fingers to the heel) as a measuring device when felting. Place the heel of one hand inside at the head opening, and your other hand outside the hat. Rub the hat twice around the head opening with plenty of soapy water. Move both hands to the next unrubbed area of the hat and rub twice around this area. Continue to measure and rub until you have covered the entire hat surface. Keep most of the hat on the work surface as you rub to prevent excess stretching of the fragile wet felt.

Squeezing Out Water

21 Gently squeeze the hat about 15 times over the rinse tub, squeezing out a little water each time. Dip the hat back into the clean, warm soapy water, squeeze out about half the water and place the hat on the worktable.

Knead and toss the hat gently, as you would bread dough, 25 times. Dip the hat back into the soapy water, then squeeze out excess water.

Throwing the Hat (Fulling)

22 The hat is now strong enough to be thrown against the tabletop. This process, which is called fulling, will speed up the felting process.

Note: A low table works best for this, giving you more room to toss. Stand with your feet shoulder width apart, relax your knees, and throw with both hands so you don't hurt your back. Raise the wet felt over your head and throw it down as hard as you can onto the table. It should make a good loud thump. Add small amounts of soapy water to the hat between tosses. A good rule of thumb is that there should be enough water in the hat to make a loud thump but not so much that you splash all over yourself. If you have a topknot on your hat, turn the hat inside out so the topknot will not continually hit you in the face. If you find throwing difficult or uncomfortable to do, try vigorously kneading the hat instead.

Throw the hat 25 times. Squeeze it a few times in the clean soapy water. Continue to throw 25 times and squeeze until the felt surface is covered with small pebbly bumps, then an additional 25 times. You'll have to throw the hat a total of 75 to 150 times, depending on how vigorously you do it.

Finishing and Sizing the Hat

23 Try the hood on the hat block. Notice that both the hat block and the felted hood are ovals (longer in the front to back length than the narrower side to side width). Match the hat block and the hood carefully. Check the fit of the hood. It probably will be larger than the hat block.

23 You're almost done felting the beret. Rinse the soap out of the hat by vigorously squeezing it under hot running water. Try on the beret. If the opening is too small, place your hands at opposite sides of the opening and gently pull. Move your hands around the opening, giving a small pull each time. Be careful, as this procedure can increase the head opening quite quickly. Enlarge the opening until the fit is comfortable. If the opening is too big, soak the beret in soapy water and throw it a few more times, or rinse it again in hot water, vigorously rubbing the head opening area until it shrinks to the correct size. Hang the beret to dry.

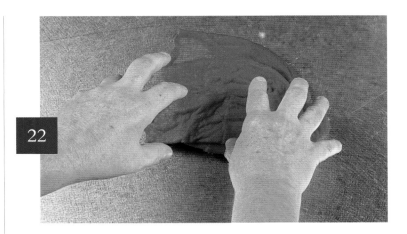

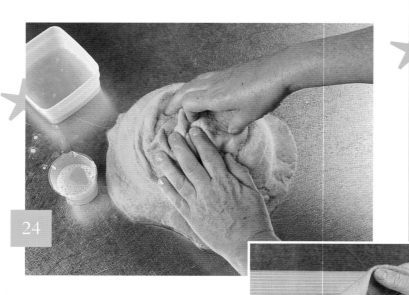

24 You'll now felt the hood to fit the hat block. Pour warm soapy water onto the crown of the hood while it's on the hat block. With your fingers, mash the hood against the block and rub your hands hard against the felt until the large wrinkles disappear. You want to rub and shrink the wool to the crown, so don't pull the brim down to fit the crown. (**Note:** The felt will shrink in the direction in which you are rubbing). You may also rub the ridged plastic container lid against the felt to shrink it. Always make sure you have enough soapy water on the felt before rubbing or you may cause pilling on the surface.

25 Remove the hood body from the hat block and lay it on the ridged felt mat. Hold the brim open with one hand and, with the ridged plastic container lid in the other hand, rub the inside of the hood very hard, moving from the brim to the very top of the crown. Rub around the hood twice.

Put the hood back on the hat block to check the fit. If the crown is still too large, repeat the rubbing with soapy water, your hands, and the ridged plastic container lid until the crown fits the hat block.

26 Take the hood off the block and repeat rubbing the inside of the hood with the ridged plastic container lid. This will firm, shorten, and strengthen the brim area. Rinse the hood vigorously under hot water. The hot water will act as a felting tool and shrink the felt more. Remember to rinse the soap off the hat block. **Note:** If possible, place the wet hood in your automatic washer and turn the dial to the final spin cycle. This will spin out much of the excess water in the hat. If the hat has a lot of dreadlocks or wings, use a final vinegar rinse to help get the soap out of them. Use 2 tablespoons (29.5 mL) of vinegar to 1/2 gallon (1.9 L) of cool water to make the rinse.

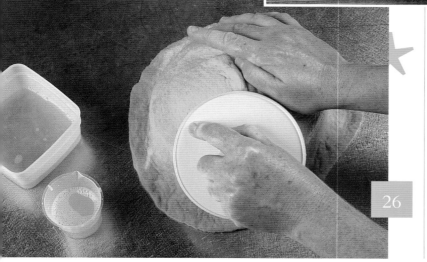

Shaping the Hood on the Hat Block

27 Place the hood on the hat block and place the hat block on top of the juice can. Pull the hood down gently to fit the crown of the hat block.

Put the large rubber band over the hood and place it halfway between the crown and the bottom of the hat block.

28 Hold the crown of the hood with one hand and pull the brim down with the other, moving around the entire hat body. When the crown fits smoothly again on the hat block, move the rubber band to the edge. The rubber band keeps the hat stretched. The juice can gives you extra room to pull the brim down. Follow the specific instructions for your project to make brims with different shapes or brimless hats.

Drying the Hat

29 Let the hat block stay in the hat body. It will dry faster if you place a fan in front of it. After 1 hour, very carefully take off the rubber band and remove the hat from the hat block. Carefully re-form the hat if needed and place it back on the juice can until it dries. **Note:** If small wrinkles refuse to be stretched out, try steaming them with an iron. Hold the iron about $^1/_4$ inch (6 mm) away from the hat block to let the steam escape. Keep your hands away from the steam for safety.

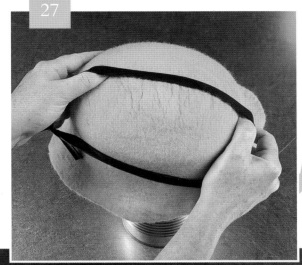

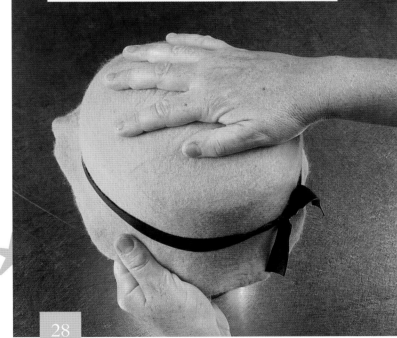

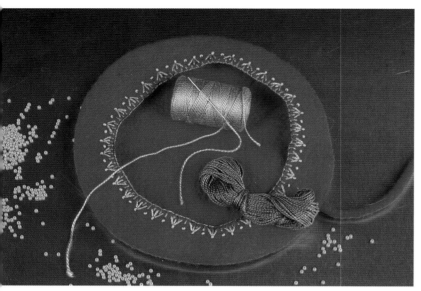

fINISHING TOUCHES

Finishing a hand-felted hat can be the most enjoyable part of the process. You've spent time and energy designing and felting your hat, and now comes the reward—trimming and embellishing your creation. You can enhance the look of even the simplest hat.

A "Healed" Edge

The head opening or brim edge of your new hat will present you with opportunities for creative decisions. You may want to leave the opening or brim as it is. But you might want to trim a few bumps or uneven areas for a smooth appearance. If you do cut the edge, either for a single bump or a major styling, you'll want to "heal" it so that all the layers and fibers felt together. You can heal cut areas by rubbing them with soapy water and your fingers until the cut edge matches the rest of the edge. Make sure to rinse off the soap afterwards. Sometimes just rubbing the wet finished felt with your fingers will be enough to heal the edge.

The trimmed and healed head opening or brim edge can present a perfect opportunity for embroidery. A buttonhole stitch (see page 65) is fabulous, as would be the addition of buttons or beads.

Bias Tape and Decorative Edging

Commercial or handmade bias-tape trim is a perfect choice for adding a striking line of color around the brim, or just giving the hat a finished look. Bias tape trim can also keep the head opening from stretching and help a large brim keep its shape. Bias tape trim is cut on the bias (or diagonal) of a woven fabric. Fabric strips cut on the bias can then stretch to go around the curves of the hat brim or crown edge without wrinkling.

Commercial bias tape is available in any store that carries sewing supplies. It's ready to use, but the color and fabric choices are limited. If you wish to use commercial bias tape, get the double-fold, extra-wide type.

Velvet ribbon, available in a range of widths and colors, is also great to use as an edging. It doesn't stretch, so use it on head openings and brims that have simple curves. The pile of velvet hides hand-stitching and small bumps.

Synthetic suede, a washable fabric made to imitate leather, makes a great edging and doesn't need to be cut on the bias. It can be purchased in small amounts. Its stretching ability varies.

Soft glove leather is a treat to use and can be the ultimate hat finish. Look for off-cuts of this material at fabric outlet shops since it can be quite expensive. Pick the very thinnest leather you can find as you'll be folding and hand-sewing it, and any extra bulk will detract from the elegance of the finish. Thin leathers can be stitched by machine with regular needles.

Handmade bias tapes are easy and fun to make, don't require a lot of material, and can be made from most types of fabrics (including patterned fabrics). On the following pages, you'll find simple instructions for making your own bias tape.

Making Handmade Bias Tape

Cut a square of fabric, any size.

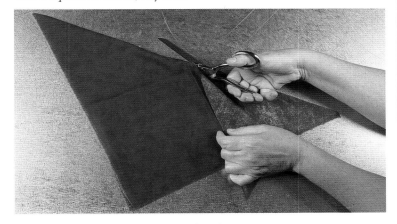

Fold your square on the diagonal and cut it corner to corner.

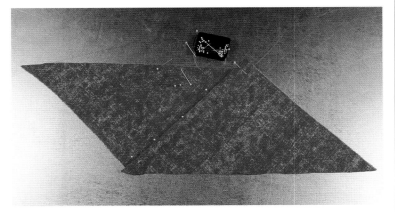

Place the triangles with right sides together, pin, and machine-stitch a ¹/₄-inch (6 mm) seam. Iron this seam open.

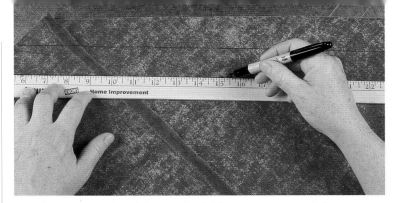

On the wrong side of the stitched fabric, measure and draw your cutting lines 2 inches (5 cm) apart, parallel to the long edges.

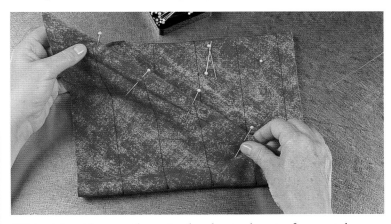

With right sides together, pin the short edges to form a tube, offsetting a 2-inch (5 cm) width in from the edge. Match the drawn cutting lines and stitch a ¹/₄-inch (6 mm) seam. Press the seam open.

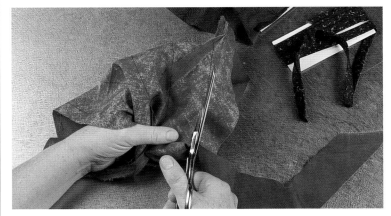

Cut the fabric on the cutting lines starting with the offset width on the edge.

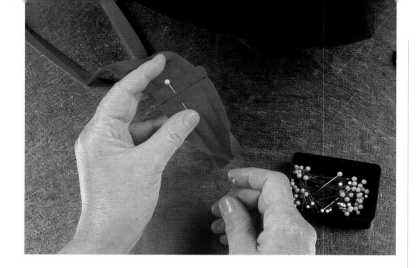

Attaching Bias Tape and Decorative Trim To Your Hat

First, make sure the hat fits well on the intended head. Then measure the head opening or brim edge. An easy way to do this is to pin the end of the trim to the brim or opening and carefully fit it around the edge, adding $^1/_2$ inch (1.3 cm) for a seam. Cut the trim and stitch right sides together with a $^1/_4$-inch (6 mm) seam.

Quarter-Pinning

An easy way to pin the trim on a hat smoothly is to mark quarter measurements on both the trim and the hat. Do this by folding the prepared trim in half and marking both ends with a pin. Open up and refold it with the two pins in the center, and mark the ends with two more pins. Now the trim is marked in quarters. Do the same to the hat opening or brim edge. Match up the pins, add additional pins, and you're ready to stitch the seam. Quarter pinning is especially helpful for making large head openings smaller. You can do this by measuring the head at the widest point, adding a 1/2-inch (1.3 cm) seam allowance. Measure and cut the trim to this size. Sew a $^1/_4$-inch (6 mm) seam on the trim or bias tape, quarter-pin, and sew it to the head opening. Iron the hat body with a steam iron to shrink it to the trim.

Note: When I sew trim on larger hat brims like the Katharine Hat (page 80), I subtract $^1/_2$ inch (1.3 cm) from the actual brim measurement before stitching. When the trim is stitched on the hat, the slightly smaller size helps create a tension on the brim, which holds the edge up or down.

The first seam will be machine-stitched and will look neater. For brimless hats and berets, pin the trim to the outside of the hat and machine-stitch a $^3/_8$-inch (9.5 mm) seam (except for velvet ribbons, which may need a much narrower seam depending on the width of the ribbon). Remove the pins and fold over the trim to the other side. Clip the trim to the hat with hem clips to hold it in place while you hand-stitch it to the other side. For brimmed hats, decide if the brim will be up or down, and what side will be seen the most. This side will be the one on which you will pin and machine-stitch the trim. When stitching sticky trims like leather or suede, turn the hat inside out so you are stitching on the felt edge.

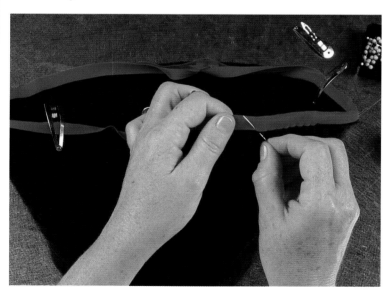

The cut points on Sophisticated Lady, Spike, and Winged Wonder are rather sharp at the front and back of the hat. To make a smooth turn at the points when machine stitching, stitch to the center point, lift the machine needle, and pivot the hat and binding. Replace the presser foot and resume stitching.

Stiffening Your Hat

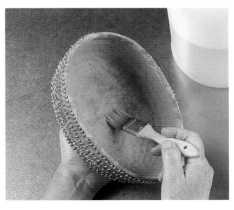

Some hat shapes and designs benefit from the addition of a stiffening agent. I used a stiffener on the inside crown of Sophisticated Lady (page 67) because without it the weight of the added brass safety pins would cause the crown to collapse on itself. I simply brushed stiffener onto the inside of the crown and placed it over the hat block to dry to help the crown maintain its shape.

The Madeline Hat needs stiffener to help its broad brim stay stiff in all types of weather. The sculptural abilities of stiffener are obvious in the Winged Wonder. The wings are stiffened and held in place with pins until they dry.

There are many different kinds of stiffeners, and each gives a different feel and finish to a hat. Experiment with several to see which one best suits your needs. Felter May Hvistendahl suggests the old Norwegian method of dipping the felt into skim milk. Hatmaker Carol Marston, who makes plastic hat blocks, uses a dry refined shellac that can be diluted with water or alcohol. You can purchase several stiffening and sizing products, including a nonhazardous water-soluble gelatin sizing, from millinary supply companies. The stiffener I used for the hats in this book is made from a confectioners glaze and mixed with 190-proof alcohol and is water-resistant. Read the manufacturer's instructions for use before applying the product you choose.

For interesting and creative results, try acrylic matte mediums (used for acrylic painting). You may find many uses for these versatile liquids. Just remember that the product you choose will change the "hand" (feel) of the felt, so consider how you want your hat to feel as well as look.

Adding a Label

After all the work you've put in to your hat, it's fun to add a tag or label with your name on it. Fabric nametags, both printed and woven, are available in different amounts, sizes, shapes, and colors from several suppliers. Some felt hatmakers create their own tags with small pieces of embroidered felt.

Name tags can either be hand-sewn to the inside of the crown or glued on with flexible fabric glue. Traditionally, the placement of the tag signified the front or back of the hat and how it was to be worn, but the felted hats in this book can be worn in almost any direction, so placement of the tag is up to you.

Caring for Your Felt

"How do I care for this hat?" is one of the questions I'm often asked. The answer will depend on the type of hat. Most of the hats in this book can be gently hand-washed in cool water in the same way one would hand-wash a wool sweater. If a hat has been stiffened or embellished with beadwork or leather trim, a drycleaner with experience in cleaning hats may be the answer. A do-it-yourself aerosol powder, available at western wear shops, can clean common water and grease-based stains.

If you're caught out in the rain or snow with your hat (which is pretty common given the purpose of hats!), simply shake off any excess water or snow and stuff the crown of the hat with newspapers. Place the hat on a waterproof surface with a towel to dry. Water will wick out of the hat and drip off the bottom.

PROJECTS

Once you know how to make a basic beret or hood, you can make an infinite variety of hats simply by altering these basic forms. Add a top-knot or dreadlocks to a beret, stretch out a hood, or add a brim to it and shape it on a round-top hat block. Your choices are limited only by your imagination. This section of the book features 15 projects, as well as ideas for variations of each. To make each project, you'll refer back to the Basic Beret and Basic Hood instructions on pages 26 through 37. The instructions for each hat project provide detailed information and how–to photos that show you how to modify the basic form you learned to achieve the new style.

THE ARTIST BERET

A classic artist beret is the perfect starter project for a beginner. This timeless design is updated with saucy red wool and a long, knotted topknot for a jaunty look. This form is just a jumping off point for many, many variations, some of which you can see on the following pages. Use your imagination to come up with your own—the sky's the limit.

■ You Will Need

Red merino roving for the beret body, 1³/4 ounces (50 g)

12-to 18-inch-long (30.5 to 46 cm) red merino roving for the topknot

Plastic resist material and beret pattern (see page 17)

Felting kit (see page 12)

Cardboard circle, 5-inch (13 cm) diameter (for the head opening template)

THERE'S MORE THAN ONE WAY TO MAKE A BERET. THIS FRENCH HATMAKER DISPLAYS A TRADITIONAL KNITTED BERET BEFORE AND AFTER FULLING.

PHOTO BY CARY WOLINSKY/IPN

45

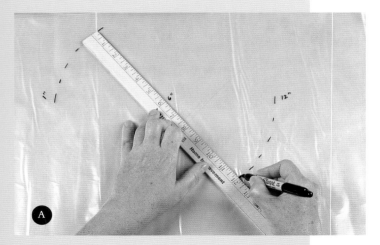

Making the Resist Pattern

A. Make a 12-inch-diameter (30.5 cm) resist pattern using the plastic resist material and following the beret pattern directions on page 19. **Note:** This size hugs the head more than the 14-inch (35.6 cm) size.

Making the Topknot

Choose the size for your topknot—anywhere between 12 and 18 inches (30.5 to 46 cm). Divide the roving in half, then in half again to make a one-quarter thick roving (see page 15). Follow the instructions on page 24 for felting the topknot.

Making the Body of the Hat

B. Follow steps 1 through 14 for the Basic Beret on pages 27 through 32. When starting step 15, add the topknot root to the center of the beret, gently pressing and rubbing the root of the topknot with additional soapy water for about 1 minute until it appears to be attached. Let the topknot lie flat while working the rest of the beret. Continue felting, following steps 16 through 23, pages 32 through 35. **Note:** Since you're using red wool for both sides of the beret, you can decide to place your topknot on either side. If you use contrasting colors of wool for each side or add prefelt designs, you'll have to decide which side of the beret will be the top and place your topknot there.

Finishing the Hat

C. Check for the correct size as explained in step 23, page 35. Flatten the beret and pull at the edges with your fingers until it has a nice round shape again. Hold the base of the topknot and pull the other end to straighten it. Tie a knot anywhere you please. You can change the placement of the knot at any time by unknotting it, soaking the wrinkled knot area, pulling it straight, and re-knotting elsewhere. Hang the beret over a clothesline until dry.

You may want to try using contrasting colors for the top and bottom of the beret. You'll see less of the batt that is wet first (in step 8) and more of the second batt placed on top (in step 11). For this beret, the first side was laid out in white and the second in black.

Try cutting a 7-inch-long (18 cm) straight cut in the center of the beret for the head hole (Basic Beret, step 18) instead of a circle. This type of opening changes how the beret sits on your head. Another idea might be to change the position of the head hole.

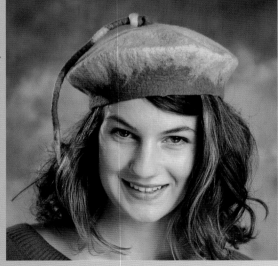

Try a resist-dye technique for this simple but sophisticated hat.

BE A STAR BERET

You'll feel like a celebrity in this stellar beret. Add prefelt stars to the top, and you'll be wearing the night sky on your head! The design combines an easy-to-make star shape body and a band. For star-gazing adults, the addition of the band gives more head room. For small children's sizes, you can make the beret without the band.

■ You Will Need

Blue merino roving for the beret body, 2 ¹/₂ ounces (71 g)

4-inch-long (10.2 cm) merino roving for the topknot in each of the following colors: yellow, red, and blue

Yellow and red merino roving for prefelt stars, ¹/₄ ounce (7 g) in each color

Blue merino roving for band, ³/₄ ounce (21 g)

Plastic resist material and Be a Star template (page 110)

Felting kit (page 12)

Cardboard circle, 5 inches (13 cm) in diameter (for the head opening template)

Sewing machine (if adding band)

Sewing kit (if adding band) (page 14)

JORIE JOHNSON
Square Berets: Moss, 2000
Fine merino 68s, assorted silk fabric selvage inlays, novelty yarns; machine stitching
PHOTO BY TSUYOSHI ITO

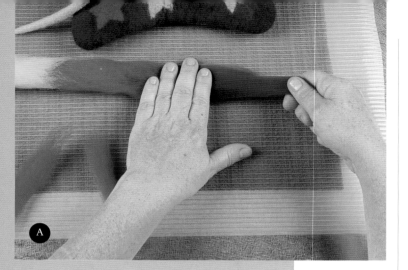

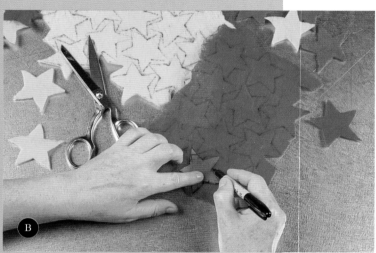

■ Making the Resist Pattern

Make the resist pattern using the plastic resist material and Be a Star template on page 110.

■ Making the Topknot

A. There will be three colors on your beret, and you'll use each color for the topknot. Lay out each 4-inch-long (10 cm) roving side by side in a 4 x 15-inch (10 x 38 cm) rectangle. Roll up the rectangle on the felt mat, continuing to roll in the same direction until the piece is firm. Keeping 3 inches (7.6 cm) of the blue roving dry for a root, wet the topknot by dribbling soapy water onto it. Saturate it by flattening it down on the mat, then pinching it back into shape. Gently roll it back and forth with open fingers until it has a good round shape. Use either your hands or the sushi mat to continue rolling the topknot until it's very firm. Follow the instructions on page 25 to finish the root end.

■ Making the Prefelt Designs

B. Use the red and yellow roving to make two 9-inch (23 cm) prefelt squares, following the instructions on page 22. Copy the star template on page 110, and with a marker and trace as many stars as you like onto the prefelt, then cut them out.

■ Making the Body of the Hat

C. Now you're ready to start making the body of the hat. Follow steps 1 through 14 on pages 27 through 32. As you lay out the layers of wool, extend the seam in the direction you are laying out the wool the same way you would if using the circular beret patterns. Feel along the resist pattern to locate the edge.

At step 4, lay out the radiating pattern on the fourth layer, starting from each of the star points moving in to the star center. Fill in the remaining wedge-shaped areas from the center out to the edges, (see photo, left).

D. When you get to steps 10 to 14 (pages 31 and 32), gently separate the wool seam where the star points start to branch out from the center. This will make it easier to fold over the seam later. Also, check the points of the star and remove any excess wool that might make them too bulky.

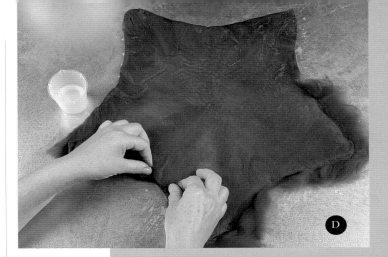

■ Attaching the Prefelt Designs and the Topknot

E. At step 15, add the topknot root to the center of the beret, gently rubbing it for about 1 minute.

The prefelt stars are placed only on the top side of the beret, around the topknot. Press down to saturate them. Make sure to save some stars to put on the band. Continue lightly rubbing and pressing the designs and topknot root area, along with the rest of the beret top, with plenty of soapy water. Follow the beret directions through step 18 (page 33).

At step 19 (page 34), use your pointer finger to reach into the star points when smoothing out the edge ridges. It may be easier to place your hand flat with the thumb in one star point and other fingers in the adjacent point when rubbing the area between the points.

Continue with the beret directions through step 23 (page 35), and hang the hat to dry.

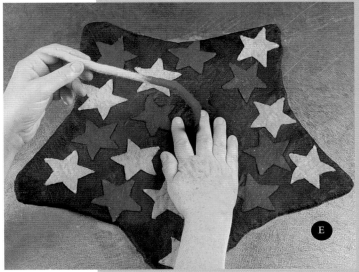

■ Making the Band

F. When you're finished with the beret body, it's time to make the band. Make a rectangular guide for laying out the wool from plastic resist material or fabric. The width of the guide will be 5 inches (13 cm), and the length will depend on the size of your head opening. Measure the head opening. Let's say it's 23 inches (58.5 cm). Since merino wool will shrink about 40 percent while felting, multiply the hat opening size by 1.40. That number will be the length of your layout guide. For this example, the guide would be 5 x 32 inches (13 x 81 cm).
Note: To measure the head opening, place a pin at one point and start measuring from that point around the circumference. The pin reminds you where you started.

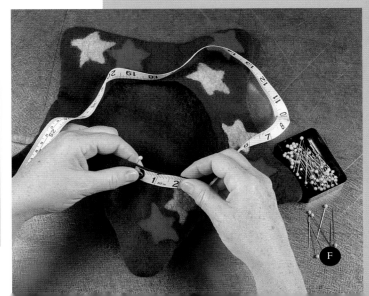

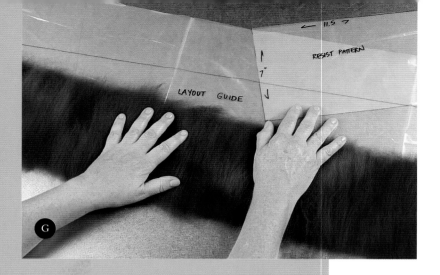

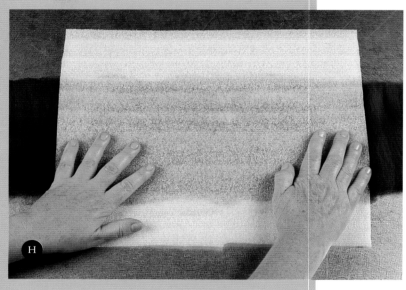

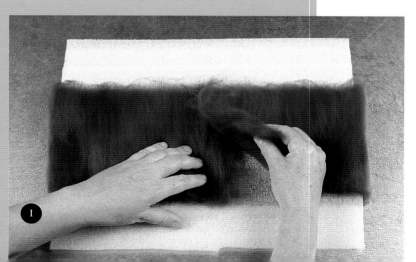

G. Lay out three layers of the blue wool reserved for the band over the layout guide. The first layer should move from the top to the bottom, the next layer left to right, and the third layer from top to bottom again. Extend the wool over the left and right sides of the guide about 1 1/2 inches (4 cm) for the seams. Dry felt the batt for 1 minute. Turn the batt over and remove the band layout guide.

H. Measure and cut out a rectangular plastic resist pattern for the band. It should be 7 inches (18 cm) high and half the length of the layout guide (7 x 16 inches [18 x 41 cm] for example).

Place the resist pattern over the center of the band. Note where the edges are and temporarily remove the resist pattern. With your dipper cup and soapy water, wet only the area that was covered by the resist. Replace the resist and press it down to saturate the wool.

I. Fold in the two dry sides over the plastic resist, letting the extended seam wool overlap in the center. Wet this area with soapy water. Add the remaining prefelt stars to both sides, and gently press and rub the band according to the Basic Beret instructions, step 15 (see page 32).

Continue to felt, moving the band around the plastic resist to eliminate and rub out the ridges at the sides. When the band becomes firmer, slip out the plastic resist and rub the band only along the length (because you want the length, not the width, to shrink). (**Note:** The direction in which you agitate or rub wet wool is the direction in which it will felt and shrink more significantly.) A quick way to shrink the band is to roll it tightly into a cigar shape, then roll it back and forth with your hands on the ridged felt mat or on a damp sponge. Continue this process for about 1 minute, then unroll and re-roll the band from the other direction.

Keep felting until the band length matches the size of the beret head opening, then rinse the band under cool water, squeeze, and flatten it. Measure again. If the length has gotten shorter than the head opening circumference, stretch the band gently to enlarge it. Straighten the edge by pulling out the bumps.

When the beret band is dry, measure and draw a straight line on the edges. Trim along your guideline, keeping as much of the band as possible.

■ Attaching the Band to the Beret Body

J. Pin the band to the head opening, right sides together, using large quilting pins. Machine-stitch the band and hat together with a $1/4$-inch (6 mm) seam and a medium stitch length. Fold the bottom half of the band inside the beret and hand-stitch it to the stitched seam you just made, butting the cut edges together to make a smooth finish. If you like, hand-stitch a grosgrain ribbon or decorative band over the stitching line.

Variation

Make the star beret all in yellow—it's a great topper for a special occasion, such as New Year's Eve.

THE QUEEN BERET

This beret style evolved from the Scottish Highland "bonnet" (traditionally worn by soldiers). For this very sophisticated style, we change the shape of the hat after it's felted and add a bias tape finish. The resulting Queen Beret folds flat for travel or storage—very convenient for those royal jaunts.

■ You Will Need

Green merino roving for the beret body, 2 ounces (57 g)

Plastic resist material and beret pattern on (see page 17)

Felting kit (page 12)

Cardboard circle, 5-inch (13 cm) diameter (for the head opening)

Iron

Bias tape (page 39)

Sewing machine

Sewing kit (page 14)

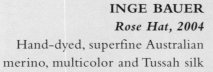

INGE BAUER
Rose Hat, 2004
Hand-dyed, superfine Australian merino, multicolor and Tussah silk
PHOTO BY ANDREAS KIENINGER

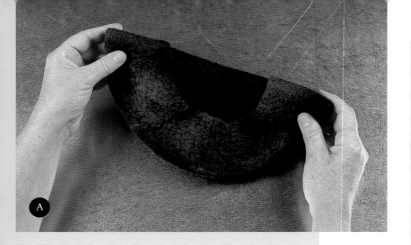

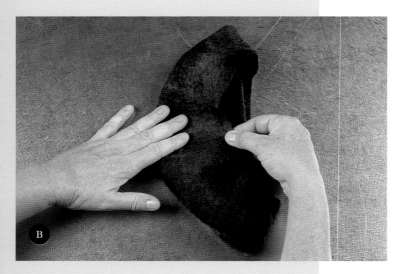

■ Making the Resist Pattern

Make a 14-inch-diameter (36 cm) beret pattern using the plastic resist material, following the instructions on page 17.

■ Making the Body of the Hat

Follow steps 1 through 14 for the Basic Beret on pages 26 through 32.

■ Shaping The Hat

A. When the beret is finished but still damp, you'll start the shaping that gives the Queen Beret its distinctive shape. With your hands, flatten the beret and tug at the edges to make it round. Fold the beret in half.

B. Pull up each side to meet the center fold. Press out the wrinkles in the bottom curve of the beret with your fingers.

C. Place your thumbs in the ends of the folds, and with your forefingers, move the fold upward and the beret sides downward so that the center fold and the two sides are even and create a straight line. The ends will become narrower.

D. Iron to press out the rest of the wrinkles and make the Queen Beret totally flat. Hang the Queen over a clothesline (or clothes hanger) to dry, centering the fold over the clothesline.

Finishing the Hat

E. Add bias-tape edging according to the instructions on page 40. A nice thin leather edge adds to the elegance of this beret shape. Or try attaching woven ribbons at the back point of the beret for a classic military look!

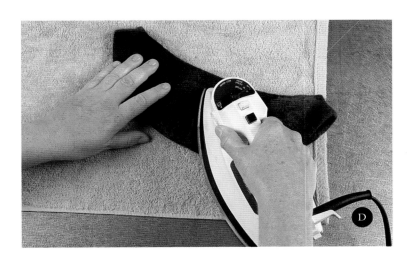

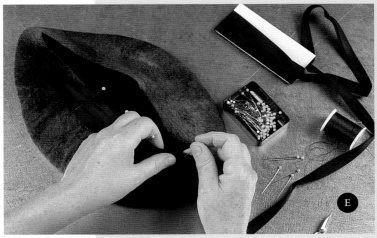

Variations

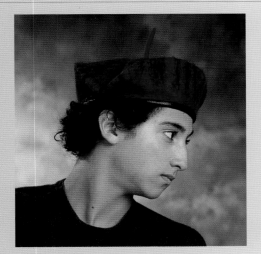

Although dyeing is outside the scope of this book, the Queen Beret lends itself nicely to resist dyeing. For this design, wooden clothespins were clamped along the new fold of the white queen hat, and the hat was dyed in a black dye bath. The clothespins will "resist" or keep the dye from penetrating where they are clamped.

To make this variation, lay out one side with 1 ounce (29 g) of red wool and the other side with 1 ounce (29 g) of black. When wetting the beret body, start with the black side. Place the top-knot on the red side, and cut the head opening on the black side.

The Queen can create infinitely different looks depending on how you place it on the head.

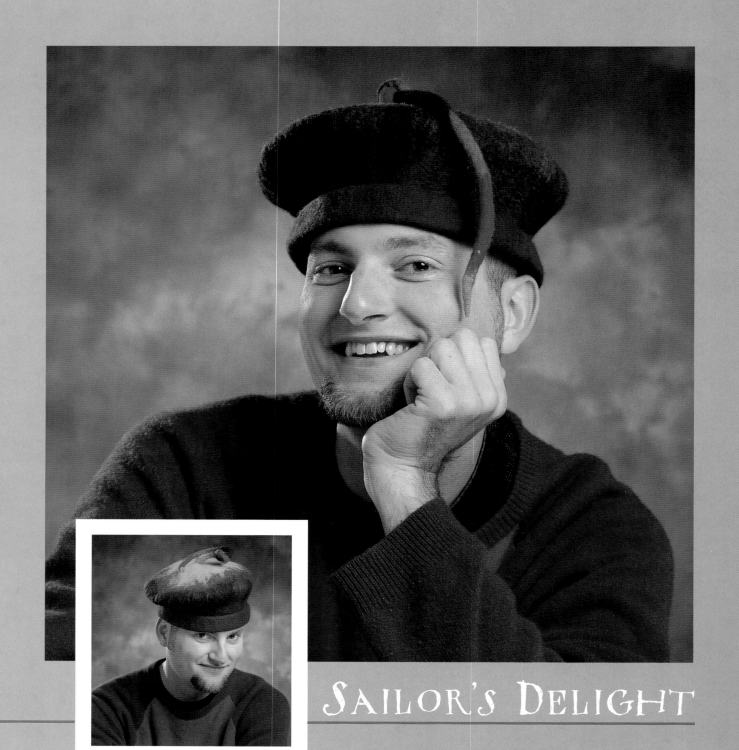

SAILOR'S DELIGHT

This charming and adventurous cap updates the classic sailor's hat with fun details, such as a radiating-color design for the beret body and the addition of a band around the head-hole opening. And, of course, where would you be without a striped topknot to tell which way the wind blows?

■ You Will Need

Blue merino roving for the beret body, 1 3/4 ounces (49 g)

Merino roving for the radiating pattern, 1/4 ounce (7 g) each of blue, yellow, orange, red, purple

12-inch-long (30.5 cm) yellow merino roving for the topknot

Blue merino roving for the band, 1/2 ounce (14 g)

Plastic resist material

Felting kit (page 12)

Fabric for band layout guide

Cardboard circle, 5-inch (13 cm) diameter (for head opening template)

Sewing machine

Sewing kit (page 14)

JACQUELINE MIRABEL
Windswept, 2004
Hand-dyed merino wool, hand-dyed
silk ruffle; silk felted into wool
PHOTOS BY STEVE FENTON

59

A

B

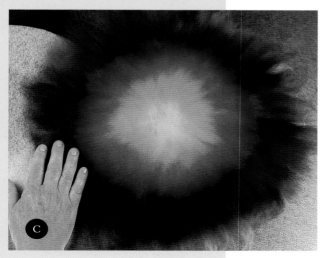

C

Making the Resist Pattern

Make a 12-inch (30.5 cm) beret resist pattern with the plastic resist material, following the directions on page 17.

Making the Topknot

A. Make a 12-inch-long (30.5 cm) striped topknot by dividing the yellow roving in half, and then in half again, so you have a one-quarter thick topknot. To make the topknot's stripes, first pull out shingles (each about 2 x 3 inches [5 x 8 cm]), from the yellow, orange, blue, red, and purple roving. Place them in a row next to each other. Place the yellow topknot in the middle of the colored strips (leave 3 inches [7.6 cm]) on the end uncovered for a root).

B. Tuck the top of the strips over the yellow roving and roll the roving toward you, rolling up the colored strips in the process. Gently roll the piece back and forth a few times to consolidate the fibers. Wet by dribbling soapy water on the topknot, keeping the 3-inch-long (7.6 cm) root dry. Saturate the topknot by flattening it on the felt mat, then pinching it back together in a round shape. Gently roll it back and forth a few more times until it regains its rounded shape. Follow the directions for felting the topknot on page 24.

Making the Body of the Hat

C. Using the blue merino roving, follow steps 1 through 3 for the Basic Beret on pages 27 and 28. For step 4, you'll be using your colors for the radiating pattern. Start laying out the yellow from the center, then move to orange, then red, purple and finally blue when you get to the edge of the batt. You'll have some wool left over, so don't try to place it all on the radiating layer.

Continue through steps 5 and 6 on page 29. For the second batt, use the blue wool for all four layers, including the radiating fourth layer.

D. When you begin step 7 (wetting the batts), make sure you start with the blue batt. By doing this, the multicolor batt will be placed on top of the blue batt (at step 11), and the radiating colors will wrap around the blue side as the seam, creating a very nice continuous color design. Continue through step 14 on page 32.

At step 15, add the yellow topknot root to the yellow center of the multicolored side, gently rubbing the root for about 1 minute. Let it just lay flat on the beret body as you work through steps 16 through 18 (pages 32 and 33).

Cut a 5-inch (13 cm) head hole in the center of the blue side of the beret for step 18. Continue felting and finishing the beret following steps 19 through 23 (pages 34 and 35). Let the beret dry.

■ Making the Band

Use the ¾ ounce (21 g) of blue wool and follow the band-making directions on page 52 and 53.

Variations

The Sailor's Delight can be made in a single color if you like. This example was made with a 10-inch diameter (25.4 cm) beret resist pattern. The band width can be changed to be either wider or narrower than 5 inches (13 cm).

Change the beret body diameter or the placement of the head hole to create different personalities. This variation is made with a 16-inch (41 cm) diameter, and the head hole is cut closer to the edge.

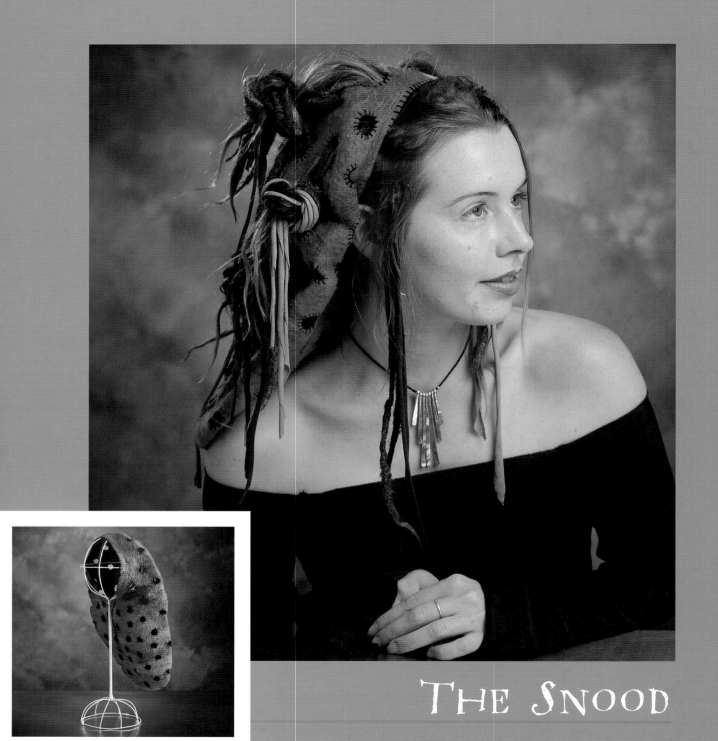

THE SNOOD

Snood is a 15th-century term for a net sack worn at the back of a headpiece to hold a woman's hair. This marvelous felted snood pays homage to the old netted version with buttonhole-stitched holes. It's great for holding dreadlocks or ponytails, or just for tucking up your hair. Use different colors inside and out and the snood becomes reversible.

■ You Will Need

Yellow and orange merino roving for the hat body, 1 ³/4 ounces (50 g) of each color

Felting kit (page 12)

Plastic resist material and Snood template (see page 109)

Cardboard circle, 5-inch (13 cm) diameter (for head opening template)

Iron

Small coin

Fine-tip marker

Sewing kit (page 14)

Pearl cotton or thin wool yarn

Large-eye sharp needle to fit choice of thread

MAY J. HVISTENDAHL
Hats for Long Haired Ladies, 2003
Hand-dyed merino wool
PHOTO BY ARTIST

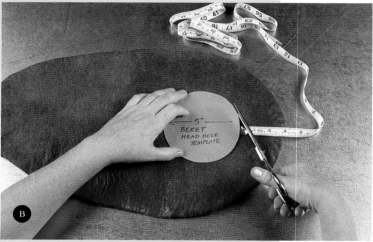

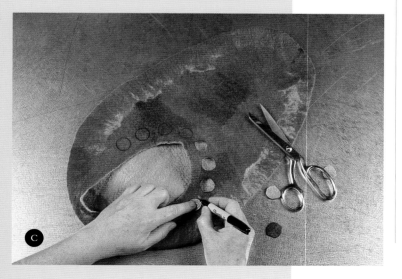

■ Making the Resist Pattern

Make the snood pattern using the plastic resist material and the Snood template, following the instructions on page 17.

■ Making the Body of the Hat

A. Follow the Basic Beret directions from steps 1 through 18 on pages 27 through 33. **Note:** For step 1, divide each color of roving into two piles—one for each side of the hat. For steps 2 through 4, use yellow for the first and second layers, and orange for the third and fourth layers (the fourth being the radiating layer). Repeat the same color sequence for the second batt. When you start step 8, make sure the orange wool (the radiating layer) is facing down, and at step 11 it's facing up.

B. At step 18, you're ready to cut a head opening. For the snood to hang down the back of your head, measure in 3 inches (7.6 cm) from the center of the narrow end of the wet felt batt. Place the edge of your 5-inch (13 cm) diameter cardboard template at this point. This is where you'll cut the head opening.

Continue with the Basic Hood instructions, steps 19 through step 23 on pages 34 and 35. When you've sized the hat opening to your head, carefully block the snood by laying it flat on the table and gently tugging the edges back into an egg shape. Iron with a cool iron and hang over a hanger to dry.

■ Finishing the Hat

C. Since hand-felted wool is a non-woven fabric, it won't unravel when cut. Take advantage of this feature by cutting small coin-sized holes all over the snood body to reveal the inside color. It's easy to get a consistent round hole shape by drawing around a coin with a fine-tip marker pen. Draw the holes and cut them out with a sharp pair of scissors.

D. Embroider around each cut hole with the buttonhole stitch and either a thick pearl cotton thread or thin yarn. You can hide the beginning and ending threads by pulling the needle and thread through the center of the thick felt for 1 inch (2.5 cm) or so, then cutting the excess thread. Stitching around the head opening (also with the buttonhole stitch) is a nice touch.

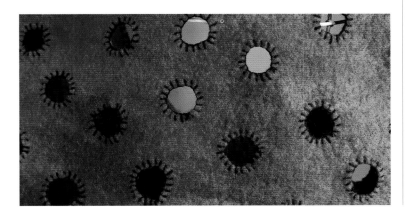

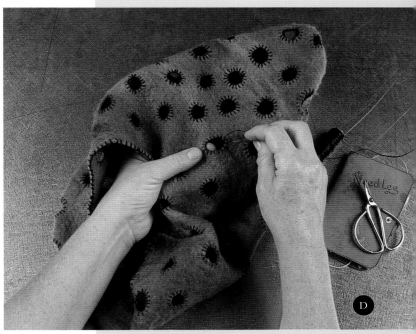

Variation

The large snood hat body gives you plenty of room to felt variegated yarns on the top layers of the wool batt, and to add fabulous antique buttons when the snood is finished.

SOPHISTICATED LADY

This fabulous faux pillbox hat with cutaway sides fits beautifully over the ears, and its back point sits nicely on the nape of the neck. Try wearing the "Lady" at a slight angle with the front point over one eye.

■ You Will Need

Gold merino roving, 1 1/2 ounces (42 g)

Plastic resist material and round-top, no brim template (page 108)

Felting kit (page 12)

Flat-top hat block

46-ounce (1.3 L) juice can

Large rubber band

Bias tape

Sewing machine

Sewing kit (page 14)

Small brass safety pins

INGE BAUER
Summer Dream, 2003
Silk organza felted with superfine
Australian merino; multicolored
and hand–dyed
PHOTO BY ANDREAS KIENINGER

67

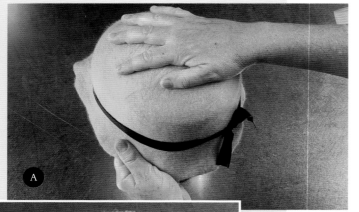

■ Making the Resist Pattern

Make a resist pattern using the plastic resist material and the round-top, no brim template (on page 108), following the directions on page 17.

■ Making the Body of the Hat

A. With the merino roving, follow the directions for the Basic Hood on pages 26 to 37, from step 1 through 29. This hat won't have a brim when finished, but there will be enough extra felt extended beyond the rubber band at step 27 for you to pull down and stretch the hood on the hat block.

B. When the hood is dry, replace it on the hat block so it fits securely. Turn the hat block upside down on the can, and trim the edge of the hat flush with the hat block edge.

C. Use some quilting pins from your sewing kit to pin the hood to the hat block in these places: close to the edge of the hat block at the front and back, and about 1 inch (2.5 cm) up from the hat block edge at the sides (halfway between the front and back pins).

■ Trimming the Brim

D. The pins will be your cutting guide for this next part. Start at the front pin and cut upwards in a curve toward the side pin (the side pin is the highest point of the cut).

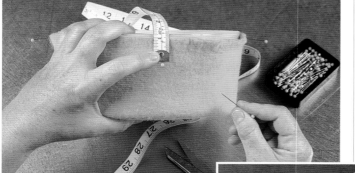

Cut down from the side pin to the back pin. Repeat for the other side. Try the hat on and see if you love it or want a deeper side cut. If you do, just move the side pins higher and cut a new curve. **Note:** For variations on this theme, try cutting the side at a different curve, or cut the back higher than the front. The placement of your guide pins determines the height and angle of the cut.

■ Finishing the Hat

E. Follow the instructions on page 40 for adding bias trim to the curved edge of a hat.

Pin rows of small brass safety pins to the hat for a truly rich look. Start by pinning a row along the bottom, just above the binding. For all the other rows, alternate placement of the pins, overlapping the rows slightly.

■ Applying Stiffener

When you've finished adding the pins, you'll need to apply stiffener to the hat, as the weight of the pins will cause the hat edges to roll inwards without it. Brush the inside of the hat body with stiffener (see page 41), and place the hat back on the hat block to dry.

E

Variations

Soft but dense felted merino is a perfect material for beadwork embellishment. The matte finish of the felt provides a nice contrast to the shiny brilliance of beads. Choose your bead colors to provide either color and/or textural contrast, or to match the felt color. When sewing on the beads, run the thread through the thick dense felt so the thread is invisible on the inside of the hat. When starting a new thread, pull the knot into the felt to secure it. When ending a thread, make a knot, pull the needle about 2 inches (5 cm) just under the surface of the felt, tug the knot into the felt, and cut off the excess thread.

BOB MARLEY TRIBUTE

Deciding how to wear the dreadlocks on this creative hat is almost as fun as making the hat! Try braiding them, wrap and tie one dread around the others, or sew beads to the ends. This is certainly a hat that will make you stand out in a crowd!

■ You Will Need

White merino roving for the hat body, 1¹/₂ ounces (42 g)

Black merino roving for the hat body, ¹/₂ ounce (14 g)

6 lengths of white merino roving for the dreadlocks, each 18 inches (46 cm) long

Black merino roving for the tips of the dreadlocks, ¹/₂ ounce (14 g)

Plastic resist material and round-top, no-brim template (page 108)

Felting kit (page 12)

Round-top hat block

Piece of plastic for flipping hat

46-ounce (1.3 L) juice can

Large rubber band

Bias tape

Sewing machine

Sewing kit (page 14)

ELINA SAARI
Adjustable Felt Lace Hat, 2004
Hand-dyed Finnish lamb's wool; felt
lace technique and traditional feltmaking; loose felt "hörhö (in front)
and felt pearls (on both sides)
PHOTO BY TOMI KALLIO

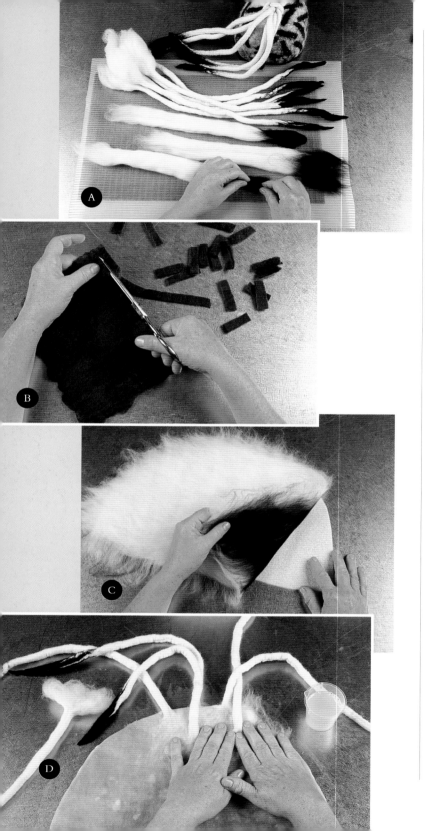

■ Making the Resist Pattern

Make a resist pattern using the plastic resist material and the round-top, no-brim template, following the directions on page 17.

■ Making the Dreadlocks

A. Take the six 18-inch (46 cm) lengths of white roving reserved for the dreadlocks and divide each length in half lengthwise. Lay out a black wool shingle on the tip of each dreadlock. Fold over the wispy top fibers and gently roll the dread to wrap the black around it.

Follow the directions on page 24 to felt the dreadlocks.

■ Making the Prefelt

B. Lay out and felt an 8-inch (21 cm) square of the black roving, following the instructions for making prefelt on page 22. Cut the prefelt into 1/2-inch-wide (1.3 cm) strips, each about 2 inches (5 cm) long. Divide the pieces into two piles, one for each side of the hat.

■ Making the Body of the Hat

C. Follow the instructions for the Basic Hood on pages 26 through 37. At step 1, divide both the white and black roving reserved for the hat body into two piles, one for each side of the hat. When laying out the layers, use black for the first layer, and divide the white into three piles, one for each of the three subsequent layers. Continue with the Hood instructions through step 6, page 29.

At step 7, place the black side of the batt facing up. Continue through step 10 (page 31).

At step 11 (page 31), place the black side of the second batt facing down so that you'll be constructing the hat body with black on the inside. When felted, the black wool will migrate to the white outside surface, creating a very nice grey color mixture. Continue with the Basic Hood instructions, steps 12 through 14 on pages 31 and 32.

D. At step 15, attach the prepared dreadlocks to the hat body. Use six dreadlocks on each side of the hat. Place the first dreadlock on the top of the hat, with one side of the root on each side of the hat. Arrange the remaining dreadlocks, some on the fold of the hat and some around the first dreadlock, spreading out the root circle of each, wetting and tapping each down with your fingertips. You may need to add more soapy water. Lay the dreadlocks facing upwards.

E. After the dreadlocks are attached to the first side of the hat, place the prefelt stripes on the wet hat body. Press down to saturate. Place a large piece of plastic over the first side of the hat before flipping it to attach the dreadlocks and prefelt stripes to the other side of the hat.

Continue with the hood directions on page 32, steps 16 through 26. This hat won't have a brim when finished, but there will be enough extra felt extended beyond the rubber band for you to pull down and stretch the hat on the hat block as described in step 27.

F. At step 27, straighten each dreadlock by holding the root end with one hand and tug it hard with the other hand.

■ Finishing the Hat

Dry the hat. Trim the edge, and attach the bias tape of your choice to the hat, following the directions on page 40.

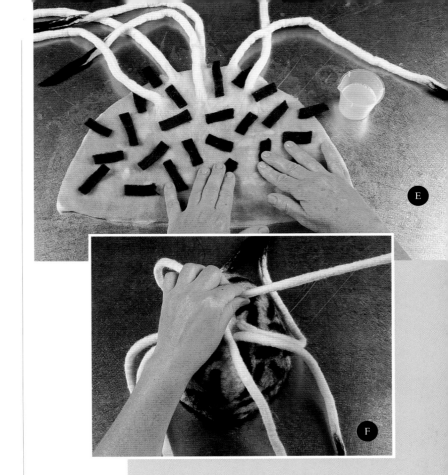

Variation

The dreadlocks on your hat can be braided, wrapped around each other and tied, or even tied with ribbons. You can curl them with dowels and rubber bands by following the directions on page 25.

Variations abound when you are designing your own dreadlocked hat. Use different colors for each dreadlock, or make them all with stripes. Make more or fewer dreadlocks. The prefelt can be made in different colors and designs. This is a very unique hat so make it uniquely yours!

SPIKE

This unusual hat looks darling on children and daring on grown-ups. Spike takes advantage of the round-top hat form to show off 160 bristling spikes. You'll need to make the hat body a bit thinner than the basic model because the root ends of the spikes cover it with another layer of wool.

■ You Will Need

*Black merino roving for the hat body,
1¹/₄ ounces (36 g)*

*60-inch-long (1.5 m) pink merino roving for
the spikes*

*20-inch-long (51 cm) gold merino roving for
the spikes*

Felting kit (page 12)

*Plastic resist material and round-top, no-brim tem-
plate (page 108)*

Large piece of plastic (for flipping the hat)

Round-top hat block

46-ounce (1.3 L) juice can

Large rubber band

Bias tape

Sewing machine

Sewing kit (page 14)

EWA KUNICZAK
Left: Sea Anemone, 2003
Right: Sea Urchin, 2004
Merino wool dyed by
artist; seamless felting
PHOTOS BY ARTIST

Making the Resist Pattern

Make a resist pattern for the round-top, no-brim hat block using the plastic resist material, following the directions on page 17.

Making the Spikes

It's best to make all of the 160 spikes at once. Divide the pink roving lengthwise into eight equal strips. Tear off 4-inch-long (10 cm) pieces from each strip. Each of the eight strips will produce 15 pieces for a total of 120 pink pieces. Divide the gold roving lengthwise into eight equal strips, and tear off 4-inch-long (10.2 cm) pieces. Each strip will produce five pieces for a total of 40 gold pieces. You now have 160 pieces for your spikes.

First, fold each spike in half, then lightly roll each a few times on the ridged felt mat until it takes on a cigar shape. Place the spikes in a neat pile.

A. Pick up five cigar-shaped spikes at a time, holding the root area (the dry bottom 2 inches [5 cm]) in your hand. Dip the tips into the soapy water and squeeze. Smush the wet tips together on your worktable (keeping the dry roots in the air).

B. This next part is a good job to do sitting down. Gather a damp sponge, the smushed spikes, soapy water, and a towel. Take each spike, dip it again in the soapy water, and roll it either against the sponge or in your hands until it's hard. Squeeze dry the spike with the towel, and put it into a new pile.

With dry hands, take each spike and tear off any excess root longer than 2 inches (5 cm). Open the rest of the dry root into a circle, as shown on page 27. Divide the spikes into two groups, one for each side of the hat.

■ Making the Body of the Hat

Make the body of the hat with the black wool, following the Basic Hood instructions, steps 1 through 14 on pages 27 through 32.

■ Attaching the Spikes to the Hat

C. The following process will help place the 80 spikes on each side of the hat. At step 15 (page 32), turn the hat body so the top faces away from you. Dry your hands and place the first gold spike on the top, with half of the root placed on each side of the hat body. Wet the root section by gently tapping it with your fingertips. You'll need to add a few drops of soapy water each time. Continue placing the spikes in rows 1 inch (2.5 cm) apart and 1 inch (2.5 cm) away from each other, wetting and tapping the roots and laying each spike on its side facing upwards when done.

Continue to place rows of spikes (moving to pink when the gold runs out), alternating the placement of each spike with the previous row. On every other row, place a spike on the outside edge of the hat body with half of the root on each side of the hat body.

D. When all the spikes on the first side are planted, spend about 4 minutes pressing them gently to start felting them to the hat body. Place five to six sponges around the hat body to absorb the excess water.

E. It's easier to flip the hat body over if you place a large piece of plastic over the finished side and flip over everything so the plastic ends up under the hat body. Use the plastic to turn the hat body on the table so the hat top again faces away from you. Place the remaining spikes on this second side, making sure that there is a spike on the edge of the hat on every alternate row.

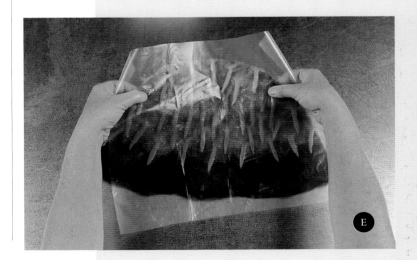

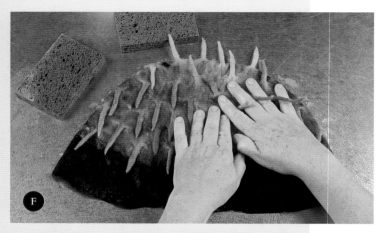

F.

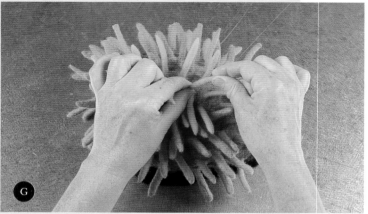

G.

Variation

There are countless color combinations for this hat, but I enjoy using small amounts of leftover wool to make dreadlocks in different colors.

F. Continue felting, following the directions on pages 32 and 33, steps 16 and 17. Press the spikes down with the rest of the hat body to move the soapy water through the wool. When you start the gentle rubbing, work from the bottom of the hat to the top, laying each spike downward as you gently rub its root area. When you reach the top, repeat the process by moving back down the hat, moving each spike upward as you rub the root area. This helps you keep track of which spikes have been rubbed and moves the other spikes out of your way. Repeat the rubbing up and down four times. Alternate with pressing down on the hat body.

At step 19 (page 34), when you take out the resist pattern and start to rub out the ridge, rub between the spikes.

Continue with steps 20 through 29, pages 34 through 37.

After step 27, you may want to use a vinegar rinse to get all the soap out of the spikes.

G. When the rinsed hat is back on the hat block and stretched with the rubber band, hold the base of each spike with one hand and pull the top with the other to stretch it out. The spikes will stay upright if they dry in that state. You may want to trim any spikes that are too long. Just rub the wet cut ends with your fingers until they're rounded again.

■ Finishing the Hat

Dry the hat and try it on. You may want to cut the edge following the directions for the Sophisticated Lady on pages 68 and 69, or just trim the bottom of the hat to the edge of the hat block. Finish with your choice of bias tape by following the directions on page 40.

JEAN HICKS
Hat Created for the Theatrical Production of
"Far Away" by Caryl Churchill, 2003
Hand-blocked and assembled merino/gotland
wool; marabou feathers

PHOTO BY JAN LOOK

HANSARD
WELSH DESIGN
Hummingbird, 2003

MAILISS PETTERSON
Daring, 2003
Merino wool and silk

PHOTO BY OLA HJELSENG

THE KATHARINE HAT

With its asymmetrical brim, this graceful hat is made for fearless, mysterious women. I've always pictured Katharine Hepburn wearing it pulled down low over one eye. The Katharine Hat is made with Norwegian Gotland wool, which creates a stiffer hat body that retains its shape through heavy weather. Directions are given for cutting an asymmetrical brim, but you can trim the brim evenly if you like.

■ You Will Need

Black Gotland batt, 3 ounces (85 g)

Plastic resist material and Katharine template (page 108)

Felting kit (page 12)

Round-top hat block

46-ounce (1.3 L) juice can

Large rubber band

Bias tape

Sewing machine

Sewing kit (page 14)

MIRIAM CARTER
Top: Gold Brim Hat with Design, 2002
*Bottom: Red Broad-Brim Hat with
Inlaid Design, 2003*
Merino wool; acid, traditional feltmaking and millinary techniques
PHOTOS BY RALPH GABRINER

■ Making the Resist Pattern

Make a resist pattern with the plastic resist material and the Katharine template (page 108) following the directions on page 17.

■ Making the Body of the Hat

Follow the directions for the Basic Hood on pages 26 through 37, steps 1 through 26.

A. Move the rubber band down to the very edge of the hat block. Turn the hat block and hat over, and place the crown on the top of the juice can. Gently fold back the brim to the rubber band. The brim fold should be even with the edge of the hat block.

B. Turn the hat and the block back over and place them on top of the juice can. If the brim seems to be too close to the body of the hat, stretch it out away from the crown. Smooth the brim with your hands so there are no odd dents or wrinkles. Let dry.

■ Cutting the Brim

C. When the hat is dry, hold it up in front of you with your hand inside the crown so you can see the lowest and highest points of the brim. Mark each of these points with a quilting pin.

D. Still holding the hat up, start cutting a gentle curve from the pin at the highest point to the pin at the lowest point, then back up to the pin at the highest point. Check and trim the edge of the brim if the curve is a bit out of line. Holding the hat up in front of you while you do this makes it easier to see the curve. Try on the hat, remembering that there really is no back or front, and see how the asymmetrical brim looks on you. Trim if needed, but remember that cutting this brim is like trying to cut an uneven chair leg. Don't go too far all at once.

■ Finishing the Hat

E. Choose your material for making the bias tape, and attach it to the hat, following the directions on page 40. For this hat, I chose a bright red bias tape, which pulls the eye to the asymmetrical shaping of the brim.

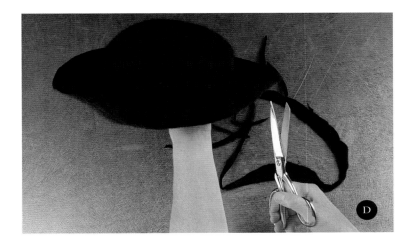

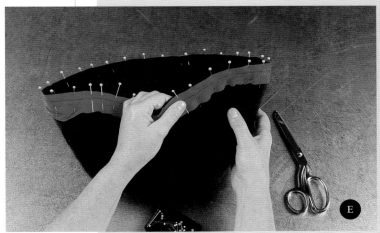

Variations

This magenta merino wool Katharine Hat features a topknot.

The Katharine has a more classic look when the brim is cut evenly on all sides.

The extra wide brim is a versatile feature—it can be worn up or down.

THE MADELINE HAT

his classic, brimmed, flat-top hat is named after the children's book character who made it her trademark. The black velvet ribbon with trailing tails evokes memories of schoolgirls, springtime, and eternal charm. The hat is made with a flamenco-shape hat block and uses felt hat stiffener to help the brim retain its shape.

■ You Will Need

Yellow merino roving, 1 3/4 ounces (50 g)

Plastic resist material and Madeline template (page 110)

Felting kit (page 12)

Flamenco-shape hat block

Large rubber band

Bias tape of your choice (optional)

Black velvet ribbon, 2 yards (1.8 m)

Sewing machine

Sewing kit (see page 14)

Hat stiffener and paintbrush

HANSARD WELSH DESIGN
Crocodile, 2003

BETH BEEDE
Over the Rainbow
(with a Nod to Minnie Pearl), 1999
Acid–dyed merino wool; form based on Zóltan Mihalkó technique
PHOTO BY ROBERT TOBEY

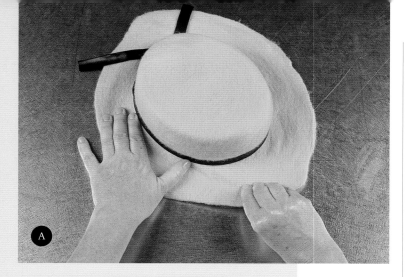

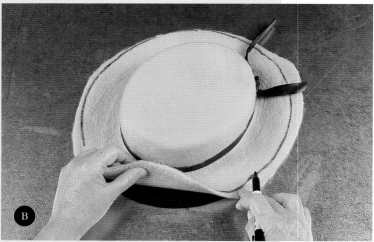

■ Making the Resist Pattern

Make a resist pattern using the plastic resist material and Madeline template (page 110), following the directions on page 17.

■ Making the Body of the Hat

Follow the directions for the Basic Hood on pages 26 through 36 from step 1 through 26.

A. At step 27, put the hat back on the flamenco hat block. Smooth and place the rubber band halfway down on the crown of the hat. Place one hand on the top of the hat, and stretch the crown downward toward the brim. After all the wrinkles have been smoothed out by the stretching, move the rubber band to the bottom of the crown.

Flatten and strengthen the brim by pulling and stretching it at a 45-degree angle to the crown.

B. You will be able to feel the plastic edge of the hat form brim under the felted wool brim. Draw a line along the brim edge with a marker, and cut along the line with scissors.

■ Finishing the Hat

C. When the hat is dry, apply a felt hat stiffener to the underside of the crown and brim. (If you are using a light-colored wool, apply the stiffener to a small area inside the hat first to see if the product discolors your hat.) Let the hat dry again.

Make your choice of bias tape edging, and sew it to the brim edge, following the instructions on page 40. Reapply stiffener as needed.

Tie a length of ribbon around the hat crown with long tails hanging down the back. Notch the ends with scissors.

If you decide not to use a bias tape edging, rub the brim edge with your fingers and warm water to heal the cut edge (see page 38). Let the hat dry.

For a humorous take on this hat, make it in black wool and attach google eyes with fabric glue.

JORIE JOHNSON
Whistling Hats Series, 2001
Natural Finnrace grays, wool fabric for hair and beard, leather cord around brim edge; stitched, felted cord decoration
PHOTO BY H. MORIMIYA

MEIKE DALAL-LAURENSON
White on White–Wedding Classic, 2000
Merino wool, silk filaments; hand-rolled felt; blocked crown; flat-wired brim; duponi silk trim; detachable white rose
PHOTO BY SIMEON JONES

WINGED WONDER

Take advantage of the superb sculptural qualities of hand-felted wool by adding extravagant wings or other appendages to your basic round-top hood. Brush-on felt hat stiffener is the secret to keeping these wings in flight. Once you've got the hang of sculpting, why not try your hand at spikes and ridges, odd circles and squares?

■ You Will Need

Blue merino roving for the hat body, 2 ounces (57 g)

Merino roving for the wings, ³/4 ounce (21 g) each of blue, red, and yellow

Plastic resist material and round-top, no-brim template (see page 110)

Plastic layout guide for wings

Cotton fabric resist

Felting kit (page 12)

Round-top hat block

46-ounce (1.3 L) juice can

Large rubber band

Bias tape

Sewing machine

Sewing kit (page 14)

Felt hat stiffener and brush

MAY J. HVISTENDAHL
Green Sea Flower, 2002
Hand-dyed merino wool
PHOTO BY ARTIST

BETH BEEDE
Georgia On My Mind, 2000
Acid-dyed merino wool and
hatter's wire; form based on
Zóltan Mihalkó technique
PHOTO BY ROBERT TOBEY

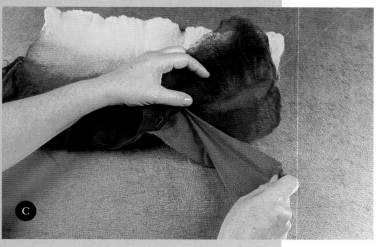

■ Making the Resist Pattern

Make a resist pattern using the plastic resist material and the round-top, no-brim template on page 108.

■ Making the Wing Guides

First, cut a plastic measuring guide to 17 x 6 inches (43 x 15 cm). You'll use this guide for laying out the wings. Next, measure and cut a 17 x 2-inch (43 x 5 cm) cotton fabric resist. This will be placed between the second and third layers of wool you lay out for each wing. The fabric resist will keep the bottom half of each wing (which will become the prefelt root which attaches the wing to the hat body) from felting together when you felt the top of the wing.

■ Making the Wings

Divide the blue, red, and yellow wool into two equal piles, one for each wing. Divide the colors for each wing into four piles for the four layers you'll lay out. The colors should be in this sequence: yellow at the top, red, then blue.

A. After you lay out the first two layers for the first wing, place the fabric resist on the lower half of the batt. Lay out the next two layers. When you've finished with the first wing, tuck in the excess wool at the sides, dry felt, and pick up the wing, putting it aside until later. Lay out the other wing on the guide in the same manner.

■ Felting the Wings

B. Felt the wings by saturating them with soapy water and then pressing and gently rubbing the soapy surface as you would do when making a prefelt (see page 22). When the entire batt is at the prefelt stage, start felting just the top of the wing (above the fabric resist) by rolling it up tightly and rolling it back and forth with your fingers on the felt mat. Continue until the top of the wing is about 14 inches (35.6 cm) in length.

■ Making the Body of the Hat

Make the body of the hat with the blue wool, following the directions for the Basic Hood on pages 26 to 32, from steps 1 through 14.

■ Attaching the Wings

C. At step 15, open up the prefelted root area of each wing by carefully removing the cotton fabric. Give the prefelt sides a tug.

D. You will be placing each wing on the hat body following a line that starts at a point 5 inches (13 cm) up from the bottom of the hat on one edge, curves to a point 3 inches (7.6 cm) down from the top of the crown, and ends at a point 5 inches (13 cm) up from the other edge of the hat. **Note:** You may want to place sponges near the hat to mark the points on the curve.

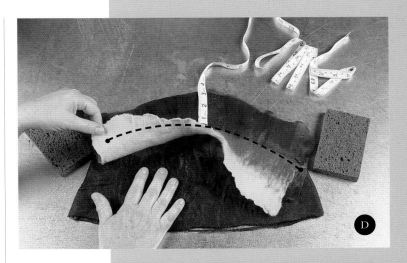

Fold the prefelted root of each wing upward toward the top felted area of the wing. Place the inner fold of the wing along the gentle curved line of the hat. Press the prefelt roots of the wing down against the hat body on both sides. Press the wing upward against the hat body, then flip over the hat, and attach the other wing following the same curved line.

Continue the felting directions for the hood on pages 32 to 37, steps 16 through 29. When you have placed the hat back on the hat block to dry, stretch out the wings by holding the base of each with one hand and pulling the wing with the other. Smooth out the wings and place them in a gentle curve.

■ Cutting and Shaping the Wings

When the hat is dry, cut the head opening, following the directions for the Sophisticated Lady on pages 68 and 69.

E. Cut and shape the wings to create your desired effect. You can trim each wing differently, if you like.

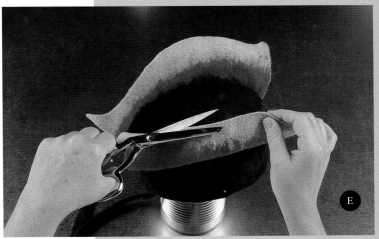

■ Finishing the Hat

F. To ensure the wings stay in the shape you want, lightly paint each wing with stiffener.

G. Arrange each wing differently, securing them in place with long quilting pins as the stiffener dries. Lightly paint the inside of the hat body with stiffener at the same time. Let the stiffener dry. Repeat if necessary.

Finish the Winged Wonder by sewing on your choice of bias-tape edging, following the directions on page 40.

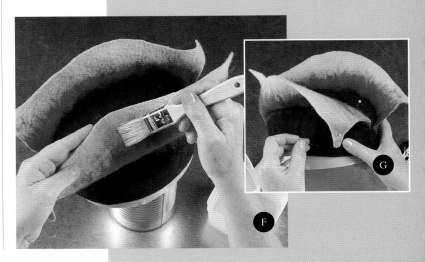

THE EXPLORER

T he bright colors of the prefelt shapes on this hat call to mind traditional Scandinavian designs. The playful topknot and practical earflaps reinterpret the look, resulting in a hat that's equally at home on an urban street corner, a ski slope, or a children's playground.

■ You Will Need

Merino roving for the hat body, 1 1/2 ounces (42 g) each of yellow and blue

Red, blue, green, and yellow merino roving for the prefelt designs, 1/2 ounce (14 g) of each

4-inch-long (10.2 cm) yellow merino roving for topknot

Plastic resist material and Explorer template (see page 108)

Felting kit (page 12)

Large piece of plastic for flipping the hat

Round-top hat block

Fine-tip marker

46-ounce (1.3 L) juice can

Large rubber band

Commercial, extra-wide, double-fold bias tape in red

Sewing machine

Sewing kit (page 14)

ALEXANDER PILIN
Hats for Carnival, 1995
Coarse, natural-colored wool;
colored embroidery
PHOTO BY PREOSSRAZENSKY

Variations

Here's another version of the Explorer made with Gotland wool on a round hat block that's shorter than the others. A buttonhole on each earflap and fancy buttons sewn to the hat crown allow you to wear the flaps up or down. There are three buttons on each side, so you have a choice of how high up you would like to adjust the earflaps. An off-center topknot completes the hat.

Made from Gotland wool and shaped on a tall dome block, this style of hat is a little longer, and features adjustable earflaps with buttons and buttonholes and a sturdy topknot to give additional distinction on your journeys.

■ Making the Resist Pattern

Make a resist pattern with the plastic resist material and the Explorer template (page 108), following the directions on page 17.

■ Making the Topknot

Make a 4-inch-long (10 cm), quarter-roving-thick topknot from the yellow wool, following the directions on page 24. Wrap a little of the blue wool reserved for the hat body around the tip of the topknot, then felt the topknot.

■ Making the Prefelt Designs

Lay out 5-inch (13 cm) squares of each of the colors for the prefelt designs. Make each square four layers thick. Follow the directions on page 22 for laying out and felting the prefelt. The designs can be cut when the prefelt is wet or dry. Cut circles, Xs, stripes, and spirals. Divide the designs into two piles, one for each side of the hat.

■ Making the Body of the Hat

A. To make the body of the hat, follow the Basic Hood directions on page 26 to 32 from steps 1 through 14. For step 1, divide the hat body wool into two piles (each half blue and half yellow). When laying out *each* layer of wool, place the yellow on the top half of the layer and the blue on the bottom half.

■ Attaching the Topknot and Prefelt Designs to the Hat

At step 15, center the topknot on the top fold. Press down half of the root on one side of the hat and saturate it, rubbing very gently for about 1 minute. Place half of the prefelt designs in a scattered pattern on this side of the hat. Press them down on the hat body to wet. Put a large piece of plastic on top of the batt, and flip everything over. Fold down the other half of the topknot root, pressing and saturating it as you did with the first half.

Place the remaining prefelt designs on this side of the hat. Press down to saturate, and continue with steps 16 through 29 (pages 32 to 37). **Note:** Place the yellow prefelts on the blue hat body and the blue prefelts on the upper yellow part. The red and green prefelts can be scattered in between the two colors.

■ Finishing the Hat

B. Open up the bias tape and iron the center fold flat. Measure the amount of bias tape you'll need by placing the tape over the line where the blue and yellow parts of the hat meet. Add $^{1}/_{2}$ inch (1.3 cm) to the measurement, and sew together in a circle with a $^{1}/_{4}$-inch (6 mm) seam. Pin the bias tape to the hat right sides together and machine-stitch on the top fold line of the bias tape. Fold the bias tape down and hand-stitch the bottom edge to the hat body.

C. Put on the hat and, with a marker and perhaps a friend, mark where the earflaps should end on your head. Mark where you want the front edge to be on your forehead, and where the back should end on your neck. Connect the marks with a smooth curving line, and trim with scissors.

D. Use more bias tape to trim the entire head opening and earflaps, attaching it to the hat, following the directions on page 40.

THE MEDIEVAL PEASANT

Oh, the timeless slouching hat! You can make countless variations of this tall, cone-shaped hat, modifying it to create whole new personalities. Use the patterns provided or design your own, featuring a smaller or taller cone-shaped top. The size and shaping of the head opening is based on the round-top resist pattern.

■ **You Will Need**

Black merino roving for the hat body, 3 ounces (85 g)

White merino prefelt batt, 20-inch (51 cm) square or white merino roving, 1 ounce (29 g)

Plastic resist material and Peasant template (page 109)

Cardboard circle, 5 inches (13 cm) in diameter

Felting kit (page 12)

Round-top hat block

Large piece of plastic (for flipping the hat)

Large rubber band

Leather bias tape

Sewing machine

Sewing kit (page 14)

JEAN HICKS
Untitled, 2004
Hand-blocked and assembled
merino/Gotland wool
PHOTO BY JAN LOOK

■ Making the Resist Pattern

Make a resist pattern using the plastic resist material and the Peasant template, following the directions on page 17.

■ Making the Prefelt Designs

A. For the striking white prefelt circle designs on this hat, use a needle-felted commercial merino batt. You can make your own prefelt batt from white merino roving (laid out in a 20-inch square [51 cm]), following the instructions on page 22. Use your cardboard circle and marker to trace 10 to 12 circles on the white prefelt. Cut out the circles and set them aside.

Making the Body of the Hat

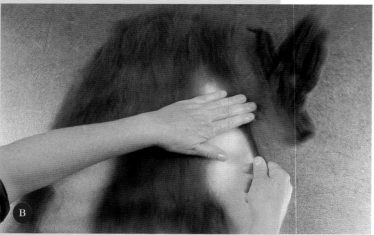

B. Follow the Basic Hood directions starting on page 26. At step 1, divide the wool for each side of the hat body. At step 2, lay out the first (and third) layers, starting with a strip of wool right down the center of the pattern and along each edge. Lay out the two side wedges with the wool shingles radiating down from the top. For the second and fourth layers, lay the wool shingles side by side. Continue with instructions for the hood through step 14, page 32.

C. At step 15, place five or six white prefelt circles on the first side of the hat body. Position some of them to wrap around to the second side. Press the circles well into the hat body to saturate. You may need to add more soapy water. Place a large piece of plastic over this side to help turn it over. Flip over the hat to the second side, and position the remaining circles. Press to saturate, and continue felting following steps 16 through 23, pages 33 through 35. You may need to rub the prefelt circles for some time before they feel securely attached to the hat. Do not poke at or pick up the edges to check on the felting. If you do, they may not reattach to the hat body.

◼ Shaping the Hat

D. At step 24 (page 35), position the hat body over the round hat block to check the size of the head opening. Rub the sides of the hat with soapy water and your hands or a ridged plastic container lid. This will shrink the sides to fit the hat block. Don't crush down the top of the hat. Continue with steps 25 through 28, page 37.

Smooth and shape the hat with your hands, pulling it into a tall, cone-shape. Place the hat back over the hat block. Use a large rubber band to secure the hat to the block. Let dry.

◼ Cutting the Brim

When the hat is dry, trim the brim evenly so that it stands upright on the table.

◼ Finishing the Hat

Follow the directions on page 39 and 40 for cutting leather bias tape strips and sewing them to the hat.

If you want the hat to slouch, rub it a while between your hands to soften the fibers. It will relax with use.

Variations

While the hat is still damp and on the hat block, crunch the center down into folds to create a striking, contemporary cocktail hat. Keep pressing the folds together and smoothing them for about 15 minutes. Keep the hat on the hat block until it's thoroughly dry. Cut the brim edge as described for the Sophisticated Lady on pages 68 and 69.

This woodland elf hat is made from green Gotland wool. The top folds over and is fastened with a decorative button.

SLICE AND DICE

Because it's a non-woven material, hand-felted wool can be cut and sliced with no worries about unraveling threads or loss of strength. The result is a stretchy and cool hat with slits that reveal the complementary color used inside. This design is made with the round-top resist pattern, and you'll use the tall or dome hat block to shape it.

■ You Will Need

Blue merino roving, 1 ounce (29 g)

Gold merino roving, 1 ounce (29 g)

Plastic resist material and round-top, no-brim template (see page 108)

Felting kit (page 12)

Tall/dome hat block

46-ounce (1.3 L) juice can

Large rubber band

Sewing kit (page 14)

Marker

Tape measure

CHARLOTTE SEHMISCH
Left: London, 2003
Right: Paris, 2004
Merino wool, synthetic dye
PHOTOS BY TINE DREFAHL

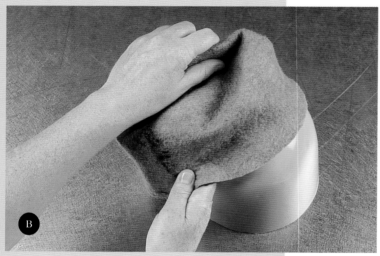

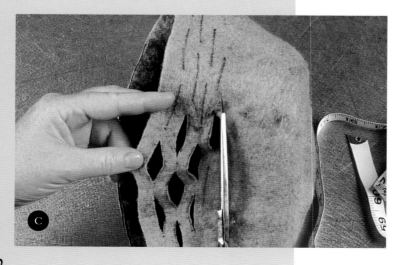

■ Making the Resist Pattern

Make a resist pattern using the plastic resist material and the round-top, no-brim template following the directions on page 17.

■ Making the Body of the Hat

A. Divide the blue and gold roving into two piles each, half the gold and half the blue for each side of the hat. Lay out the wool for the first side of the hat, with blue for the first and second layers and gold for the third and fourth layers. Repeat the same sequence for the second side.

B. Follow the directions for the Basic Hood on pages 26 to 37, from steps 1 through 26. When you're ready for step 27, place the hood on the tall dome.

Place the rubber band at the very edge of the hat block. Use the juice can under the hat block to give you more height to stretch the felt. With one hand on top of the block, gently stretch the felt below the rubber band until all the wrinkles are gone and the hat fits the tall dome block perfectly.

Carefully take off the rubber band, and let the hat dry for about 1 hour. Trim the felt to 1 inch (2.5 cm) below the edge of the hat block. Remove the hat block.

■ Cutting the Slits

C. You'll be cutting the hat while it's still damp, but not dripping wet. Use the marker to draw a 1¹/₂-inch long (3.8 cm) cutting line for your first slit, ¹/₂ inch (1.3 cm) up from the head opening. Cut along the line. Draw the second cutting line ¹/₂ inch (1.3 cm) from the first one. Continue marking and cutting 1¹/₂-inch-long (3.8 cm) slits, ¹/₂ inch (1.3 cm) apart around the hat for the first row. After the first row you will be able to visually estimate the length of the slits and the spaces in between. Continue to cut slits up to the top of the hat. **Note:** Try drawing the pattern first on paper and cutting it to get a feel for it before you try it on the hat.

To keep the length of the slits consistent, as the top part of the hat gets narrower, try creating a solid band, then resume cutting the slits in the same length, but not in the same sequence.

■ Refelting the Hat

D. When the cuts are finished, refelt the hat by dunking it back into the warm soapy water (add more hot water to your soap solution if it has gotten cold). Squeeze the hat 25 times over the waste water tub, then throw it 25 times. Put the hat back into the warm water, and squeeze some water out and throw it again 25 times. Rinse the hat in hot water. Put it back on the hat block and stretch it as far as it will go. Let dry overnight or in front of a fan. Since the refelting has healed the bottom opening and the slits, you don't need a binding.

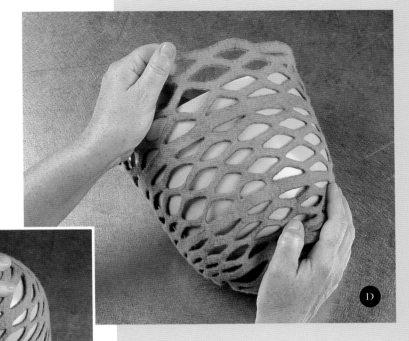

Variation

Many hats that just didn't turn out well can be rescued by this cutting and styling method. Just cut, refelt, and stretch.

THE MARVELOUS MITRE

A friend brought me a traditional hat like this from Turkey, thinking it was made from wool felt. Upon closer inspection, I discovered that it wasn't made of felt at all, but some sort of upholstery fabric. But I loved the design and have seen many hand-felted hats made in this shape. It's a variation on the bishop's mitre—a classic design used for centuries in many cultures.

■ You Will Need

White merino commercial prefelted batt, 20-inch (51 cm) square, or white merino roving for the hat body, 3 ounces (85 g)

Felting kit (page 12)

Cutting template (see page 109)

³/4-inch-wide (2 cm) velvet ribbon, 1¹/2 yards (137 cm)

Sewing machine

Sewing kit (page 14)

Note: This hat is very quick and fun to make because we're using commercially made merino prefelt. (You can quickly outfit the entire family!) You can also make prefelt by laying out merino roving, as we do for the other hats in the book.

A traditional fez is worn by "whirling dervishes," in spiritual dance rituals.
PHOTO COURTESY OF BETH BEEDE

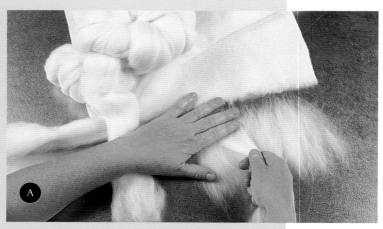

■ Felting the Prefelt Batt

A. If you're using the merino roving, divide the wool into four equal piles, one for each of the four layers. Lay out the four layers in a 20-inch (51 cm) square and felt according to the directions for making prefelt on page 22. Continue with the following directions.

B. Soak the prefelt batt (either handmade or commercial) in the warm soapy water for 10 minutes. Squeeze it gently over the wastewater bucket 15 times, squeezing out a small amount of water each time. Dip the batt back into the warm soapy water and squeeze out most of the water. Alternate kneading the batt 25 times and tossing it 25 times, dipping it into the soapy water between each process. Continue until the felt measures as a 13-inch (33 cm) square. Rinse the batt vigorously under hot water. Squeeze out as much water as you can.

C. Roll up the damp felt in a small reed mat or sushi mat to "iron" out wrinkles and shrink it a bit further if needed. Roll the felt several times in each direction. If the corners are stretched out, roll them diagonally on the mat to shrink them. Hang the felt to dry.

■ Cutting the Pattern

D. Trace the cutting pattern on page 109 and cut it out. Carefully trace the pattern four times onto the felt with a marker. Cut out the four pieces. It's helpful to pin numbers 1 to 4 to the four pieces of felt to help with assembly. (Use a ⅛-inch (3 mm) seam and a medium-length stitch.) **Note:** This size pattern fits a 23-inch-diameter (58.5 cm) head. Increase or decrease the bottom width of the pattern pieces for other sizes.

■ Sewing the Pieces

E. Pin piece #1 and the velvet ribbon, right sides together. Do the same to piece #3.

F. Pin and stitch section #2 to the other side of the ribbon which was sewn to section #1. Do the same to pieces #3 and #4.

G. With right sides together, pin and stitch a longer piece of ribbon to the other side of the sewn sections #1 and 2.

H. Pin and stitch the other side of the ribbon to the sewn sections #3 and 4.

I. Measure the head opening, add ½ inch (1.3 cm), and cut that length of velvet ribbon. Sew the ribbon ends together with a ¼-inch (1.3 cm) seam. Pin the right sides of the ribbon and hat together at the head opening and stitch. Turn the velvet ribbon to the inside and hand-stitch.

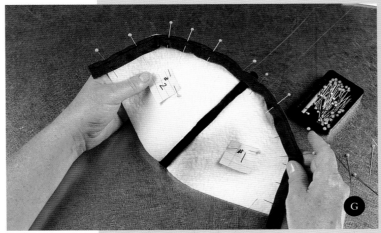

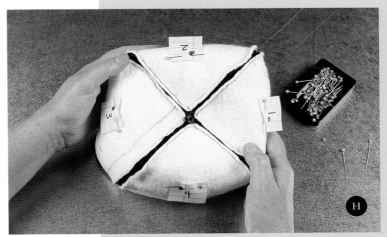

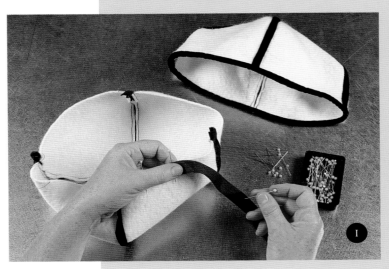

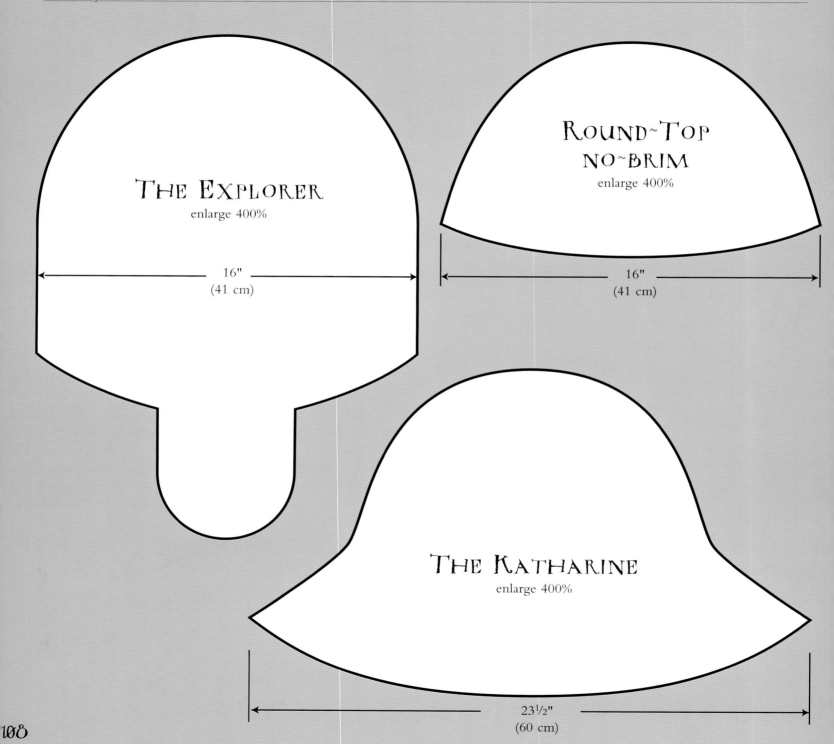

The Explorer
enlarge 400%

16"
(41 cm)

**Round-Top
no-brim**
enlarge 400%

16"
(41 cm)

The Katharine
enlarge 400%

23½"
(60 cm)

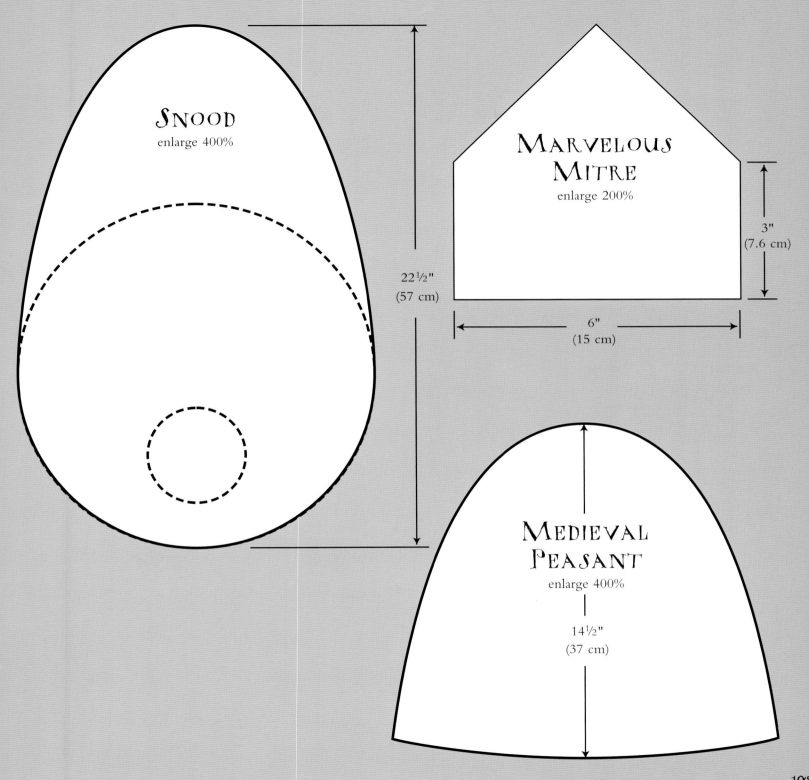

SNOOD

enlarge 400%

22½"
(57 cm)

MARVELOUS
MITRE

enlarge 200%

3"
(7.6 cm)

6"
(15 cm)

MEDIEVAL
PEASANT

enlarge 400%

14½"
(37 cm)

109

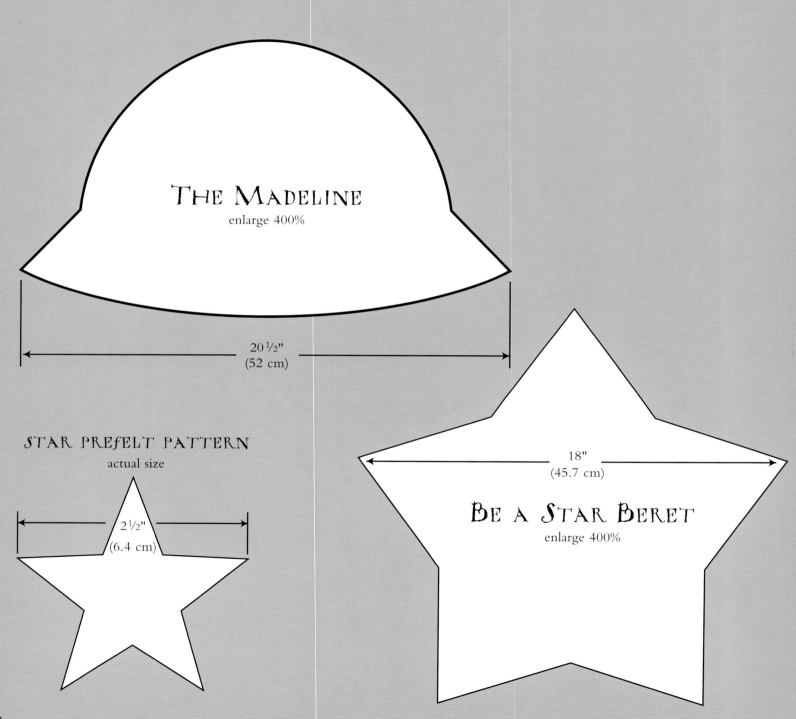

THE MADELINE

enlarge 400%

20 ½"
(52 cm)

STAR PREFELT PATTERN

actual size

2 ½"
(6.4 cm)

18"
(45.7 cm)

BE A STAR BERET

enlarge 400%

Acknowledgments

Writing a book has to be a labor of love, but working on a book on any aspect of felting is very labor intensive! As I labored through the hat designs (felting all of them several times), typed with two fingers, wrote to friends for slides, and removed cats from the computer keyboard, my head was filled with thoughts of teaching felt hatmaking to hundreds of students. Many times during workshops, I've been asked if I minded giving all my information and patterns to participants. I always answer that I've learned just as much, if not more, from my students. Seems like more than a fair trade to me!

And so it is to all those hat and felting students that I dedicate this book. And to master hatmaker Jean Hicks, whom I first met when she was a felting student, but now acknowledge as a teacher. Also, to all the fabulous felters with whom I have become good friends: Joke Van Zinderen, Inge Bauer, May Jacobsen Hvistendahl, Loyce Erickson, Jorie Johnson, Meike Dalal–Laurenson, Alexander Pilin, and Sharon Costello, among many, many others. And to those felt masters who have much to teach me, Beth Beede and Karen Page.

Also so many thanks to those feltworthy friends who encouraged me during the writing process, the Voorhees family, especially Millie, Jane, David, Molly, and Susan; my email mentor, Bhakti Ziek; the two Helens, Helen Purdum and Helen Church; my editor, art director, and photographer at Lark Books, and always to my adorable and loyal cats, Sweet Pea and Stinky, who have loved me through good food and bad.

Bibliography and Resources

Hat History

Pufpaff, Suzanne, *Nineteenth Century Hat Maker's and Felter's Manuals*. 1995. Self-published

(A wonderful reading journey into some of the early history of felt hat-making.) Available from author through www.yurtboutique.com.

Penny Mc Knight, *Stockport Hatting*. 2000, Stockport MBC, Community Services Division, Stockport, UK. ISBN 0 90516484 9

Felt

Sjoberg, Gunilla P. *Felt: New Directions for an Ancient Craft*. Interweave Press, Colorado 1996. ISBN 1 883010 17 9

Burkett, Mary, *The Art of the Feltmaker*. 1979 4 Abbot Hall Art Gallery, Kendal, UK. ISBN 0-9503335 1

Places

The Museum of Hatting, Wellington Mill, Wellington Road South, Stockport SK3 0EU, England www.stockportmbc.gov.uk/heritage/hatworks.htm

Contemporary Feltmaking

North American Felter's Network and Newsletter
Pat Spark
1032 SW Washington St. Albany, OR 97321
541-926-1095
spark@peak.org
www.peak.org/~spark/felt/feltmakers.html

Echoes, The Journal of the International Feltmakers Association www.feltmakers.com

About the Author

Chad Alice Hagen has taught feltmaking to adults and children since 1984. Her hand-felted wool has been exhibited throughout the world, and her work is included in the collections of the

Mint Museum of Art+Design (Charlotte, North Carolina), The Minneapolis Institute of Art, the University of Wisconsin-Madison, the corporate collections of B.F. Goodrich and Westinghouse, and in private collections. Hagen received her BA in Art and Master's in Textile Design from the University of Wisconsin-Madison, and her MFA from Cranbrook Academy of Art. She is the author of *The Weekend Crafter: Feltmaking (Lark Books 2002).*

PHOTO BY GABRIELLE DIETZEL

Supplies

Usually, the supplies you need for making the projects in Lark books can be found at your local craft supply store, discount mart, home improvement center, or retail shop relevant to the topic of the book. Occasionally, however, you may need to buy materials or tools from specialty suppliers. In order to provide you with the most up-to-date information, we have created a listing of suppliers on our Web site, which we update on a regular basis. Visit us at www.larkbooks.com, click on "Craft Supply Sources," and then click on the relevant topic. You will find numerous companies listed with their web address and/or mailing address and phone number.

Index

Batt, defined, 9

Basic beret and hood, instructions, 26

Beret pattern, making, 17

Bias tape,
    making, 39
    attaching, 40

Felting kit, 12

Fulling, defined, 9

Gotland, 9

Hat blocks, 14

Healed edge, 38

Hood pattern, making, 17

Laying out wool, 19

Merino, 9

Plastic resist patterns, 16
    making, 17

Prefelt,
    defined, 9
    making, 22

Roving, defined, 9

Soap, 10

Soap gel, making, 10

Soapy water, making, 11

Shingle, defined, 9

Sewing kit, 14

Specialty tools, 13

Super soap solution, making, 11

Topknots, making, 24

Wool, types of, 8